make a
Quilt in a Day®
log cabin pattern

Eleanor Burns

a Quilt in a Day® publication

To Grant and Orion
The light side of my life

1998: Fourth Edition
Sons Grant (left) and Orion (right)
with "grandpuppy" Tabitha, still enjoy-
ing the first quilt I ever finished.

1978: First Edition
Sons Grant (right) and
Orion (left) sleeping under
my early experimental quilts.

Fourth Edition: First printing June, 1998
©1998 by Eleanor A. Burns Family Trust
Third Edition: ©1986
Second Edition: ©1979
First Edition: ©1978 Eleanor Burns & William Burns

Published by Quilt in a Day®, Inc.
1955 Diamond St. San Marcos, CA 92069

ISBN 0-922705-98-4

Editor Eleanor Burns
Art Director Merritt Voigtlander
Production Assistant Robin Green

Table of Contents

1 Introduction 4

2 Measuring & Choosing A Pattern 8

3 Fabric & Color Selection .9

4 Yardage & Cutting Charts 14

5 Cutting Techniques 28

6 Sewing the Blocks 30

7 Previewing the Quilt Top 50

8 Sewing the Quilt Top Together 60

9 Borders & Backing 66

10 Choosing How to Finish Your Quilt 69

11 Quick Turn and Tie Method 73

12 Machine Quilt and Bind Method 79

13 Log Cabin Tote Bag 86

14 Log Cabin Pillow with Ruffle 90

15 Pillow Shams 92

Introduction

History of the Log Cabin Quilt

The Log Cabin design dates back to pioneer days and is one of the most popular quilting patterns. Most Colonial homes had one or more of these quilts. Completed tops were often hand quilted by neighbors welcoming a new family while all the men raised the barn.

The block is symbolic of life itself. The center square, traditionally red, represents the heart or hearth of the home. The strips around the center square are said to represent the logs of the cabin. The light side of the block represents the sun in front of the cabin. Compare "the light side" to babies, weddings, family, and friends. The dark side of the block represents the shadow behind the cabin, such as death, divorce, or disaster. The "dark" moments in life help us realize how wonderful the "light" moments really are!

By turning the log cabin blocks in different directions, many looks can be created. One design has been appropriately named Barn Raising. The Fields and Furrows layout illustrates the highs and lows of the newly plowed field. The Windmill layout is symbolic of the farmer's power source.

A light moment at the Burns household! The wallhanging appeared in the second edition of the Log Cabin book.

A partial delivery from my first 1,000 printed books.

I originally wrote this book in 1978 so anyone could be successful when making a quilt. Little did I know I had a million dollar idea! When I first began teaching quilting, I was trying to make quilts the way Grandma and Aunt Edna did… with scraps of clothing and feed sacks, scissors, and templates.

Now, with these easy assembly-line sewing techniques and updated tools, Quilt in a Day brings the possibility of making a quilt to every one. Even though our log cabin quilts are stitched together quickly by machine with fabric purchased new, they are just as warm and unique as any the pioneers painstakingly made with carefully saved scraps.

This book carries a warning with it…

…Caution: This technique is habit forming. You may never cook or clean again. But it is good for your well-being.

Enjoy the light side of life!

Eleanor Burns

5

My mother and father, Erma and Erwin Knoechel from Zelienople, Pennsylvania, gave me my first sewing machine in 1957. It was a toy hand crank Singer, and it never worked quite right, but it was perfect for sewing doll clothes for my beloved walking doll, Cindy Sue. The next year, a traveling salesman sold my mother a green Elna sewing machine, and from that decisive day, I have had a love affair with Elna sewing machines.

In 1975, after teaching special education for a number of years in the Pittsburgh school system, my husband Bill moved our family from Pennsylvania to California, and entered law school. To help support us, I turned back to my childhood love of sewing crafts and secured a job teaching Patchcraft through the Carlsbad Parks and Recreation program.

With two young sons, Grant only four years old, and Orion just a toddler, I did not have the time to dedicate to traditional quilting methods, and neither did my students. I began experimenting with quick sew techniques, often at night while my sons were sleeping. Some nights, the quilts turned out, some nights they didn't, until I developed a consistent method with assembly-line sewing techniques. I made my very first quilt top while burning the midnight oil. Would you believe it still isn't finished?

Consequently, my students and I started turning out Log Cabin quilts with beautiful results in 10 to 16 hours total time. Bill encouraged me to write down the methods I was teaching to my students. I wrote out concise, step-by-step directions, and he typed them on a Selectric typewriter and drew detailed illustrations. When he needed a model for a hand, he simply held his out and drew it. We photocopied those books as needed for students in quantities of 25 or 50, and felt pretty smug about it all!

When our marriage failed, I was left to support and raise my sons alone. With a leap of faith, I had the book

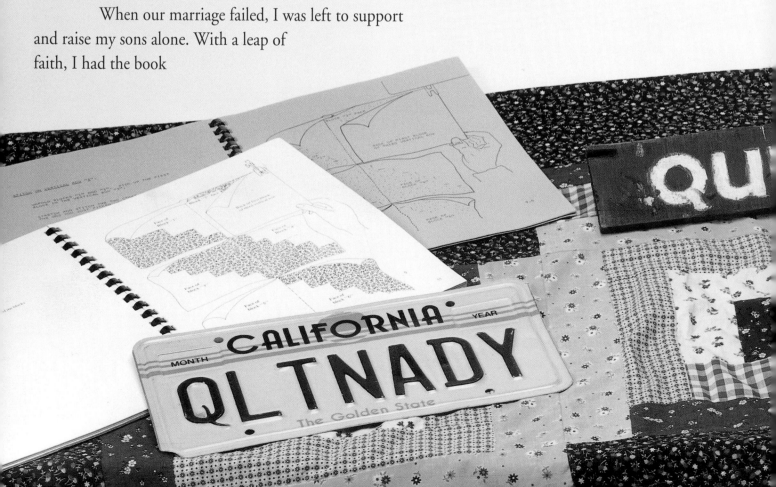

typeset by a professional, Pam Nedlik. She also improved the illustrations, substituting a slender female hand for the original drawing of Bill's hand. I cautiously purchased 1,000 books for my first printed order, worrying that perhaps I would have to store 800 books in my garage the rest of my life! Like an eager puppy, I was delighted and shocked each time I ran to the mailbox and found an order for a Quilt in a Day book.

Today, a million copies later, I'm still delighted! Judging from the number of classes and students I have had in these last twenty years, I am certain that everyone has a log cabin quilt on their beds. In my wildest dreams, I visualize an archaeological dig a hundred years from now filled with log cabin quilts. As the quilts are lovingly pulled from the dig and examined, the archaeologists will say, "This was the Eleanor Burns era!"

I hope you soon discover how much pleasure you receive from making these quilts, and how much your family will appreciate them. This is the book that got me started. Use it as the inspiration to learn an extremely useful and pleasurable craft!

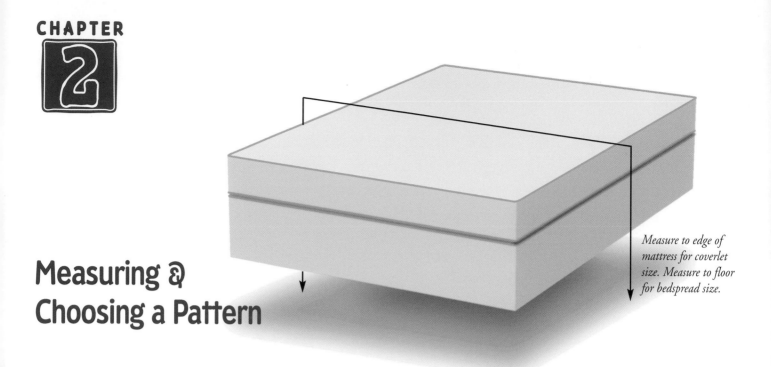

Measure to edge of mattress for coverlet size. Measure to floor for bedspread size.

Measuring & Choosing a Pattern

Decide if you want your quilt to be coverlet size, and only cover the top mattress, or to be bedspread size, and cover to the floor. Decide if you will tuck the pillows in or use pillow shams on top of the quilt.

Measure the length and width of what you want covered on your bed.

The size of the finished Log Cabin block is 14" square. Divide the length and width by 14" to help decide how many blocks you need. On most bed size quilts, the blocks cover the top mattress, the first border frames the mattress, and the remaining borders hang over the sides. Check the approximate finished sizes at the top of each yardage chart to find the one that is suited to your purposes. Single sizes are given for a baby, lap, and wallhanging. Two different sizes are given for the twin, double, queen, and king quilts.

The photos will give you some ideas as to the different styles or patterns that are possible. Not all are represented. If you want a particular pattern, check the layouts on pages 52 – 59 so you know how many blocks to make to get that particular finished look. For instance, you are limited in patterns for the baby, lap, and twin, since these sizes are only three blocks across. More patterns are possible with four blocks across, as in the sixteen block wallhanging. See that your desired pattern can be made in your size.

Fabric & Color Selection

Select 42" – 45" wide 100% cotton fabrics in calico prints. Vary the scale of the prints to add interest to your blocks.

Choose two dominant colors that compliment each other and accent the room the quilt is intended for. Decide which will be called the light color and which will be called the dark color. In this example, the light is beige, and the dark is green. There is a dramatic color difference or contrast between the lights and the darks. With the beige fabrics all the same color value, the pattern will be well defined.

Choose three different degrees of colors for each, plus a center square color. The center square color should be a solid color, or one that reads solid, found in most of the prints you choose. For example:

Center Square: Red large scale print

First Light: Light Cream small scale print

Second Light: Medium Beige small scale print

Third Light: Dark Beige large scale print

First Dark: Green and Beige tones in large scale print

Second Dark: Green with Red in medium scale print

Third Dark: Dark Green Print that reads solid

The colors should walk or move gracefully from one color into the next. In the example case, the Darks are picking up some colors used in the Lights and Center Square. Avoid choosing a very dark color for the Third Light strip because it detracts from the appearance of the quilt and confuses the pattern. The Third Light and the Third Dark should look attractive beside each other.

Choosing Borders and Binding

Be creative when choosing borders for your Log Cabin. Making the first border from the Center Square fabric helps to frame the quilt and tie the colors together. The second and third borders can be chosen from the Lights or Darks. One large scale print makes an interesting border. Binding is typically made with the same fabric as the last border or the Center Square fabric. It's not necessary to purchase binding for quick turn quilts. Remember, these are suggestions, not rules! Borders and backing can be made from any complimentary fabric, whether or not it is contained in the blocks.

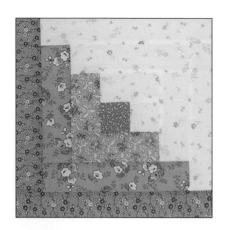

One Color Repeat

Some quilters choose to use the same fabric repeated three times on one side. In this example, the light side is a One Color Repeat. See the yardage charts for the fabric needed to make One Color Repeat blocks for your size quilt. If you need to figure how much yardage to buy, add up the total number of strips needed. Multiply the number of strips by 2½". Divide 36" into that number for the yardage amount, plus a little extra.

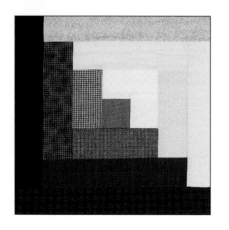

Using Scrap Fabrics

You may choose to make your Log Cabin with scrap fabrics. Choose the size quilt you would like to make, and refer to the total number of strips needed for your Lights and Darks under the One Color Repeat Chart. Arrange your scrap strips from light to dark. To keep the scrappy look, use each fabric only once in a block instead of twice.

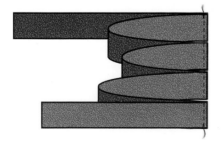

Piecing Strips

If you end up short of strips for one color, assembly-line sew them together before you start making the blocks. You waste little when you have one long strip. You can also assembly-line sew short pieces together into a long piece to get the length you need. Don't worry about seams in the strips. You'll be carrying on a proud tradition! Many antique Log Cabins have seams within the strips, as pioneer women made do with the fabric they had.

Batting

Use only bonded batting for the interior of the quilt. It has been sized so that it won't fall apart and will stay in one piece through washings. If you are not sure what you are buying, bonded batting may be identified by its strength and is tough to pull apart.

Polyester Batting

Cotton Batting

Wool Batting

Polyester Batting

Select **thin, 100% cotton batting or thin 3 ounce polyester** batting if you plan to machine quilt. If you plan to quick turn and tie your quilt, use thick, 6 oz polyester batting. Polyester batting is also recommended for baby quilts or other quilts that will be washed frequently. Polyester batting should be tied or machine quilted approximately every 4".

Cotton batting is thinner but heavier than polyester batting. Despite its density, cotton batting breathes nicely. Most cotton battings need to be machine quilted every 3" or less.

Wool batting is both warm and light, and feels wonderful to the touch. It is easy to machine quilt, as it rolls up compactly. Washable wool batting such as Hobbs Heirloom® brand can be machine quilted up to 3" apart.

Backing

Your backing fabric should be the same quality as the fabric used in the top. A sheet or a poor quality backing fabric will not have the same thread count as the quilt fabrics, which may cause uneven shrinkage when the quilt is laundered. Backing fabric can be muslin, a print or solid color used in the quilt top, or a complimentary color. You may also use scraps of all the top fabrics, although it is easier to work with large pieces of fabric.

White and muslin fabrics for backing can be found up to 120" wide, while some print fabrics can be found up to 90" wide. If you use 42" wide fabric for your backing, you must divide the fabric into two or three equal lengths and piece it together.

Shopping List

General Tools

☐ Fiskars Rotary Cutter & 6" x 24" Ruler

or
Fiskars Craft Cutter

☐ 6" x 6" Ruler

☐ 16" Square Up

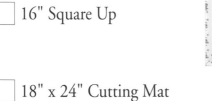

☐ 18" x 24" Cutting Mat

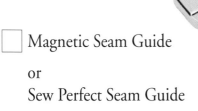

☐ Magnetic Seam Guide

or
Sew Perfect Seam Guide
or
¼" Foot

☐ Stiletto

☐ Quilter's Straight Pins

☐ 1" Safety Pins

☐ Neutral Thread

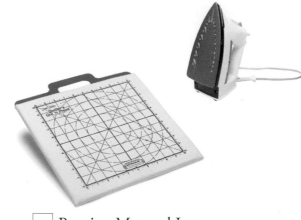

☐ Pressing Mat and Iron

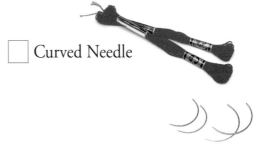

For Quick Turn and Tie Finish:

☐ Embroidery Floss

☐ Curved Needle

For Machine Quilting Finish:

☐ Walking Foot

☐ Invisible Thread

☐ Kwik Klip™

☐ Marking Pencil or Hera Marker

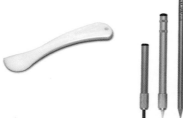

Paste-Up Sheet

This worksheet will help you keep your color selection organized. Feel free to photocopy *this page only* of the book for use with your future Log Cabin quilts. Cut a sample off your fabrics and pin or glue the appropriate fabric to the worksheet. The actual finished size of the block is 14" square.

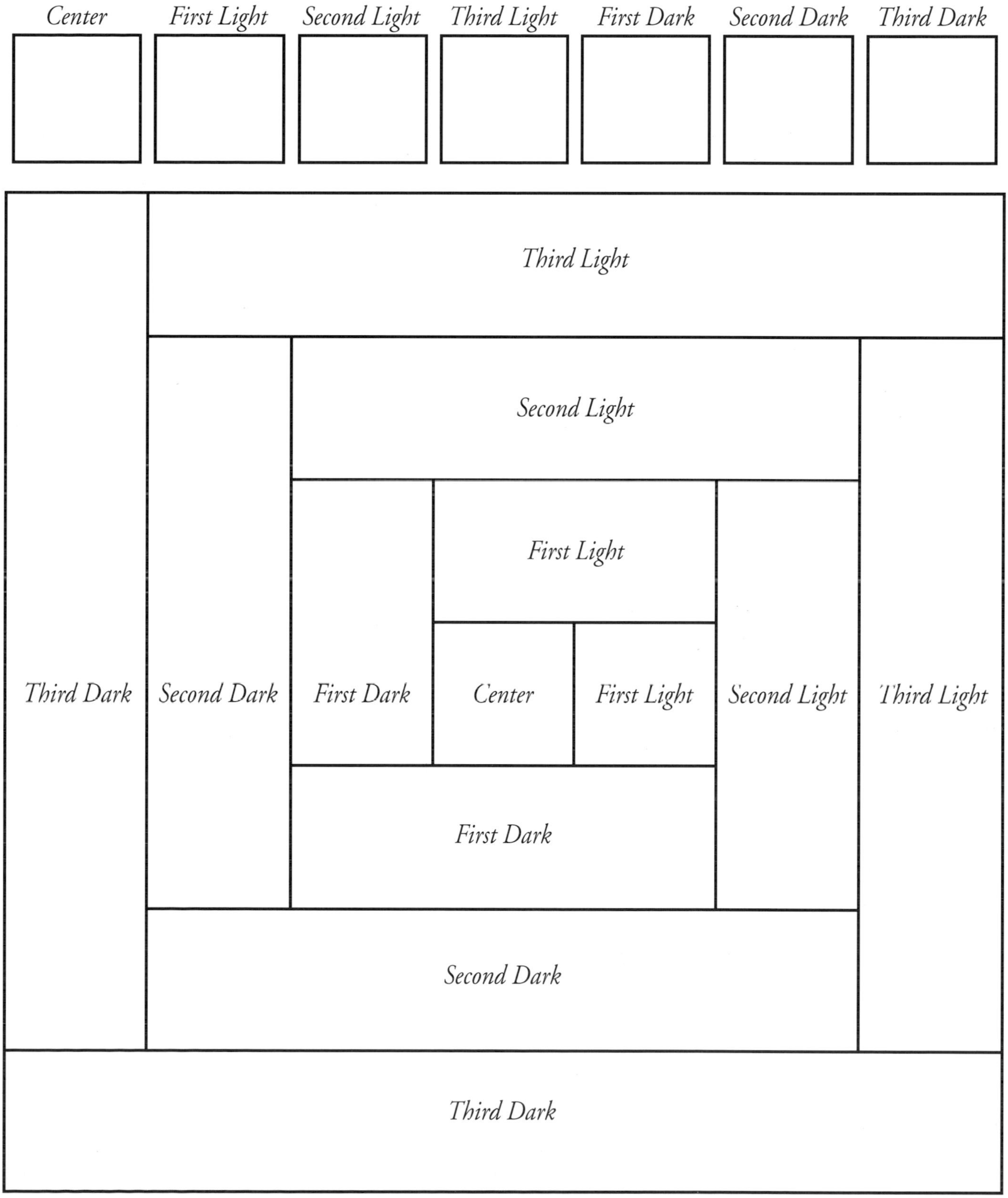

Center	*First Light*	*Second Light*	*Third Light*	*First Dark*	*Second Dark*	*Third Dark*

Third Light

Second Light

First Light

Third Dark | *Second Dark* | *First Dark* | *Center* | *First Light* | *Second Light* | *Third Light*

First Dark

Second Dark

Third Dark

Yardage and Cutting Charts

The charts on the following pages give the yardage you need for your blocks, borders, batting and backing. Each fabric is cut into the number of strips and widths needed for the blocks and the borders. All strip lengths are selvage to selvage. See cutting instructions on pages 28 and 29.

Quilt by Luckie Yasukochi

If you are finishing with a Quick Turn, binding fabric is not necessary.

If you are planning to make the All Sevens layout, a good choice for Baby, Lap Robe, and Twin sizes, purchase ½ yd extra of Third Dark. See page 51.

Finished measurements are approximate. Individual seam allowances, thick batting and extensive quilting change the approximate size.

Baby

3 Across, 3 Down
54" x 54"

Block Yardage

9 Blocks...

	Center Square	1st Light	2nd Light	3rd Light	1st Dark	2nd Dark	3rd Dark
Yardage	⅛ yd	¼ yd	⅜ yd	⅝ yd	⅓ yd	½ yd	⅝ yd
Cut Strips	(1) 2½"	(2) 2½"	(4) 2½"	(6) 2½"	(3) 2½"	(5) 2½"	(6) 2½"

or 9 One Color Repeat Blocks

	Center Square	Light	Dark
Yardage	⅛ yd	1 yd	1⅛ yds
Cut Strips	(1) 2½"	(12) 2½"	(14) 2½"

Finishing

	1st Border	2nd Border	Batting	Backing	Binding
Yardage	⅝ yd	¾ yd	58" x 58"	3¼ yds	⅝ yd
Cut Strips	(5) 2" or 3"	(6) 4"		(2) equal pieces	(6) 3"

Lap Robe

3 Across, 4 Down
54" x 68"

Quilt by Betty Bird

Block Yardage

12 Blocks...

	Center Square	1st Light	2nd Light	3rd Light	1st Dark	2nd Dark	3rd Dark
Yardage	⅛ yd	⅓ yd	½ yd	⅔ yd	⅜ yd	⅝ yd	⅔ yd
Cut Strips	(1) 2½"	(3) 2½"	(5) 2½"	(7) 2½"	(4) 2½"	(6) 2½"	(8) 2½"

or 12 One Color Repeat Blocks

	Center Square	Light	Dark
Yardage	⅛ yd	1¼ yds	1½ yds
Cut Strips	(1) 2½"	(15) 2½"	(18) 2½"

Finishing

	1st Border	2nd Border	Batting	Backing	Binding
Yardage	⅝ yd	1 yd	58" x 72"	4 yds	⅔ yd
Cut Strips	(5) 2" or 3"	(7) 4"		(2) equal pieces	(7) 3"

Wallhanging

4 Across, 4 Down
68" x 68"

Quilt by Patricia Knoechel

Block Yardage

16 Blocks...

	Center Square	1st Light	2nd Light	3rd Light	1st Dark	2nd Dark	3rd Dark
Yardage	⅛ yd	⅓ yd	⅔ yd	⅞ yd	½ yd	⅔ yd	1 yd
Cut Strips	(1) 2½"	(3) 2½"	(7) 2½"	(10) 2½"	(5) 2½"	(8) 2½"	(12) 2½"

or 16 One Color Repeat Blocks

	Center Square	Light	Dark
Yardage	⅛ yd	1⅝ yds	1⅞ yds
Cut Strips	(1) 2½"	(20) 2½"	(25) 2½"

Finishing

	1st Border	2nd Border	Batting	Backing	Binding
Yardage	⅔ yd	1 yd	72" x 72"	4¼ yds	¾ yd
Cut Strips	(6) 2" or 3"	(8) 4"		(2) equal pieces	(8) 3"

Regular Twin

3 Across, 5 Down
Coverlet: 63" x 91"
Bedspread: 74" x 102"

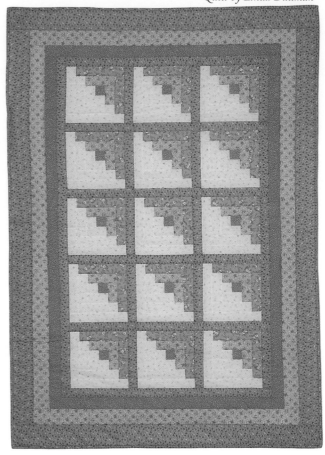

Quilt by Linda Dallman

Block Yardage

15 Blocks...

	Center Square	1st Light	2nd Light	3rd Light	1st Dark	2nd Dark	3rd Dark
Yardage	⅛ yd	⅓ yd	⅝ yd	¾ yd	½ yd	⅔ yd	⅞ yd
Cut Strips	(1) 2½"	(3) 2½"	(6) 2½"	(9) 2½"	(5) 2½"	(7) 2½"	(10) 2½"

or 15 One Color Repeat Blocks

	Center Square	Light	Dark
Yardage	⅛ yd	1½ yds	1¾ yds
Cut Strips	(1) 2½"	(18) 2½"	(22) 2½"

Finishing

Coverlet

	1st Border	2nd Border	3rd Border	4th Border	Batting	Backing	Binding
Yardage	¾ yd	1 yd	1¼ yds		67" x 95"	6 yds	¾ yd
Cut Strips	(8) 3"	(8) 4"	(8) 5"			(2) equal pieces	(8) 3"

Bedspread

	1st Border	2nd Border	3rd Border	4th Border	Batting	Backing	Binding
Yardage	¾ yd	1 yd	1¼ yds	1¾ yds	78" x 106"	6½ yds	1 yd
Cut Strips	(8) 3"	(8) 4"	(8) 5"	(10) 6"		(2) equal pieces	(9) 3"

Extra Long Twin

3 Across, 6 Down
Coverlet: 63" x 105"
Bedspread: 74" x 116"

Quilt by Teresa Varnes

Block Yardage

18 Blocks...

	Center Square	1st Light	2nd Light	3rd Light	1st Dark	2nd Dark	3rd Dark
Yardage	¼ yd	⅜ yd	⅔ yd	1 yd	½ yd	¾ yd	1 yd
Cut Strips	(2) 2½"	(4) 2½"	(7) 2½"	(11) 2½"	(5) 2½"	(9) 2½"	(12) 2½"

or 18 One Color Repeat Blocks

	Center Square	Light	Dark
Yardage	¼ yd	1¾ yds	2 yds
Cut Strips	(2) 2½"	(22) 2½"	(26) 2½"

Finishing

Coverlet

	1st Border	2nd Border	3rd Border	4th Border	Batting	Backing	Binding
Yardage	¾ yd	1⅛ yds	1½ yds		67" x 109"	6½ yds	⅞ yd
Cut Strips	(8) 3"	(8) 4"	(9) 5"			(2) equal pieces	(9) 3"

Bedspread

	1st Border	2nd Border	3rd Border	4th Border	Batting	Backing	Binding
Yardage	¾ yd	1⅛ yds	1½ yds	1¾ yds	78" x 120"	7 yds	1 yd
Cut Strips	(8) 3"	(8) 4"	(9) 5"	(10) 6"		(2) equal pieces	(10) 3"

Regular Double

4 Across, 5 Down
Coverlet: 77" x 91"
Bedspread: 88" x 102"

Block Yardage

20 Blocks...

	Center Square	1st Light	2nd Light	3rd Light	1st Dark	2nd Dark	3rd Dark
Yardage	¼ yd	⅜ yd	⅔ yd	1 yd	⅝ yd	¾ yd	1⅛ yds
Cut Strips	(2) 2½"	(4) 2½"	(8) 2½"	(12) 2½"	(6) 2½"	(9) 2½"	(14) 2½"

or 20 One Color Repeat Blocks

	Center Square	Light	Dark
Yardage	¼ yd	1⅞ yds	2¼ yds
Cut Strips	(2) 2½"	(24) 2½"	(29) 2½"

Finishing

Coverlet

	1st Border	2nd Border	3rd Border	4th Border	Batting	Backing	Binding
Yardage	¾ yd	1 yd	1½ yds		81" x 95"	6 yds	⅞ yd
Cut Strips	(7) 3"	(8) 4"	(9) 5"			(2) equal pieces	(9) 3"

Bedspread

	1st Border	2nd Border	3rd Border	4th Border	Batting	Backing	Binding
Yardage	¾ yd	1 yd	1½ yds	2 yds	92" x 106"	9 yds	1 yd
Cut Strips	(7) 3"	(8) 4"	(9) 5"	(10) 6"		(3) equal pieces	(10) 3"

Extra Long Double

4 Across, 6 Down
Coverlet: 77" x 105"
Bedspread: 88" x 116"

Quilt by Luckie Yasukochi

Block Yardage

24 Blocks

	Center Square	1st Light	2nd Light	3rd Light	1st Dark	2nd Dark	3rd Dark
Yardage	¼ yd	½ yd	¾ yd	1¼ yds	⅔ yd	1 yd	1¼ yds
Cut Strips	(2) 2½"	(5) 2½"	(9) 2½"	(14) 2½"	(7) 2½"	(11) 2½"	(16) 2½"

24 One Color Repeat Blocks

	Center Square	Light	Dark
Yardage	¼ yd	2⅛ yds	2½ yds
Cut Strips	(2) 2½"	(28) 2½"	(34) 2½"

Finishing

Coverlet

	1st Border	2nd Border	3rd Border	4th Border	Batting	Backing	Binding
Yardage	¾ yd	1¼ yds	1½ yds		81" x 109"	6 yds	⅞ yd
Cut Strips	(8) 3"	(9) 4"	(10) 5"			(2) equal pieces	(9) 3"

Bedspread

	1st Border	2nd Border	3rd Border	4th Border	Batting	Backing	Binding
Yardage	¾ yd	1¼ yds	1½ yds	2 yds	92" x 120"	10½ yds	1 yd
Cut Strips	(8) 3"	(9) 4"	(10) 5"	(10) 6"		(3) equal pieces	(10) 3"

Queen

4 Across, 6 Down
Coverlet: 83" x 111"
Bedspread: 97" x 125"

Block Yardage

24 Blocks...

	Center Square	1st Light	2nd Light	3rd Light	1st Dark	2nd Dark	3rd Dark
Yardage	¼ yd	½ yd	⅞ yd	1¼ yds	¾ yd	1 yd	1¼ yds
Cut Strips	(2) 2½"	(5) 2½"	(9) 2½"	(14) 2½"	(7) 2½"	(11) 2½"	(16) 2½"

or 24 One Color Repeat Blocks

	Center Square	Light	Dark
Yardage	¼ yd	2⅛ yds	2½ yds
Cut Strips	(2) 2½"	(28) 2½"	(34) 2½"

Finishing

Coverlet

	1st Border	2nd Border	3rd Border	4th Border	Batting	Backing	Binding
Yardage	1 yd	1½ yds	1⅞ yds		87" x 115"	6½ yds	1 yd
Cut Strips	(8) 4"	(10) 5"	(10) 6"			(2) equal pieces	(10) 3"

Bedspread

	1st Border	2nd Border	3rd Border	4th Border	Batting	Backing	Binding
Yardage	1¼ yds	1¾ yds	2¼ yds	3 yds	101" x 129"	11¼ yds	1 yd
Cut Strips	(8) 4½"	(10) 5½"	(10) 6½"	(12) 7½"		(3) equal pieces	(11) 3"

Square Queen

6 Across, 6 Down
Coverlet: 89" x 89"
Bedspread: 100" x 100"

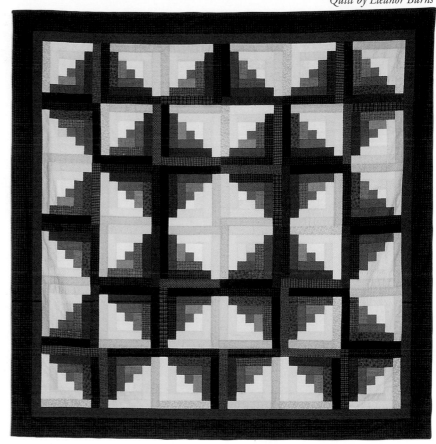

Block Yardage

36 Blocks...

	Center Square	1st Light	2nd Light	3rd Light	1st Dark	2nd Dark	3rd Dark
Yardage	⅓ yd	⅝ yd	1⅛ yds	1⅝ yds	⅞ yd	1⅜ yds	1⅞ yds
Cut Strips	(3) 2½"	(7) 2½"	(14) 2½"	(21) 2½"	(11) 2½"	(17) 2½"	(24) 2½"

or 36 One Color Repeat Blocks

	Center Square	Light	Dark
Yardage	⅓ yd	3⅛ yds	3⅞ yds
Cut Strips	(3) 2½"	(42) 2½"	(52) 2½"

Finishing

Coverlet

	1st Border	2nd Border	Batting	Backing	Binding
Yardage	⅞ yd		93" x 93"	9 yds	⅞ yd
Cut Strips	(9) 3"			(3) equal pieces	(9) 3"

Bedspread

	1st Border	2nd Border	Batting	Backing	Binding
Yardage	1⅛ yds	2 yds	104" x 104"	10 yds	1 yd
Cut Strips	(9) 4"	(10) 6"		(3) equal pieces	(10) 3"

King One

5 Across, 5 Down
Coverlet: 97" x 97"
Bedspread: 111" x 111"

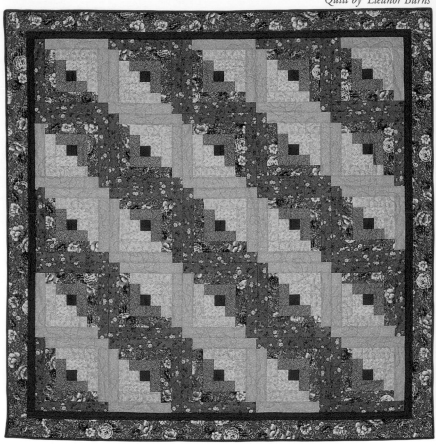

Block Yardage

25 Blocks...

	Center Square	1st Light	2nd Light	3rd Light	1st Dark	2nd Dark	3rd Dark
Yardage	¼ yd	½ yd	⅞ yd	1¼ yds	⅔ yd	1 yd	1½ yds
Cut Strips	(2) 2½"	(5) 2½"	(10) 2½"	(15) 2½"	(8) 2½"	(12) 2½"	(18) 2½"

or 25 One Color Repeat Blocks

	Center Square	Light	Dark
Yardage	¼ yd	2⅜ yds	2⅞ yds
Cut Strips	(5) 2½"	(30) 2½"	(38) 2½"

Finishing

Coverlet

	1st Border	2nd Border	3rd Border	4th Border	Batting	Backing	Binding
Yardage	1 yd	1¼ yds	1⅞ yds		101" x 101"	9 yds	1 yd
Cut Strips	(8) 4"	(8) 5"	(10) 6"			(3) equal pieces	(10) 3"

Bedspread

	1st Border	2nd Border	3rd Border	4th Border	Batting	Backing	Binding
Yardage	1¼ yds	1¾ yds	2⅜ yds	3¼ yds	115" x 115"	10½ yds	1 yd
Cut Strips	(8) 4½"	(10) 5½"	(12) 6½"	(12) 7½"		(3) equal pieces	(11) 3"

King Two

6 Across, 6 Down
Coverlet: 105" x 105"
Bedspread: 111" x 111"

Block Yardage

36 Blocks...

	Center Square	1st Light	2nd Light	3rd Light	1st Dark	2nd Dark	3rd Dark
Yardage	⅓ yd	⅔ yd	1⅛ yds	1⅝ yds	1 yd	1⅓ yds	1⅞ yds
Cut Strips	(3) 2½"	(7) 2½"	(14) 2½"	(21) 2½"	(11) 2½"	(17) 2½"	(24) 2½"

or 36 One Color Repeat Blocks

	Center Square	Light	Dark
Yardage	⅓ yd	3⅛ yds	3¾ yds
Cut Strips	(3) 2½"	(42) 2½"	(52) 2½"

Finishing

Coverlet

	1st Border	2nd Border	3rd Border	Batting	Backing	Binding
Yardage	1 yd	1⅓ yds	1⅞ yds	109" x 109"	10 yds	1 yd
Cut Strips	(9) 3"	(10) 4"	(12) 5"		(3) equal pieces	(11) 3"

Bedspread

	1st Border	2nd Border	3rd Border	Batting	Backing	Binding
Yardage	1⅓ yds	1⅞ yds	2¼ yds	115" x 115"	10 yds	1 yd
Cut Strips	(10) 4"	(12) 5"	(12) 6"		(3) equal pieces	(11) 3"

Measurements
for One Block

Center Square	2½" Square
First Light	2½" Square 2½" x 4½"
Second Light	2½" x 6½" 2½" x 8½"
Third Light	2½" x 10½" 2½" x 12½"
First Dark	2½" x 4½" 2½" x 6½"
Second Dark	2½" x 8½" 2½" x 10½"
Third Dark	2½" x 12½" 2½" x 14½"

Size, not including ruffle: 14" Square

Log Cabin Tote Bag _____

Finished Block	(See measurements above)
Bonded Batting	(1) 18" x 32" Piece
Coordinating Fabric	⅞ yd Cut (2) 17½" squares for back Cut (2) 2" x 14½" strips for sides Cut (2) 5" x 26" strips for straps
Lining Fabric	⅝ yd Cut (2) 16 x 17½" pieces
Velcro	2" length

Log Cabin Pillow _____

Finished Block	(See measurements above)
Bonded Batting	(1) 16" square
Pillow Back	⅓ yd Cut (2) 10" x 14½" Pieces
Ruffle	⅜ yd Main Fabric Cut (3) 3" Strips ⅜ yd Accent Fabric Cut (3) 4" Strips
Pillow Form	(1) 14"
Heavy Cord	4½ yds

Size, not including ruffle: 18½" x 31½"

Pillow Sham

Two Finished Blocks per Sham	(See measurements on previous page) *Buy multiples of yardage for additional sham; one sham holds one pillow.*
Borders	¼ yd Cut (3) 3" Strips
Ruffle	⅔ yd Main Fabric Cut (7) 3" Strips ⅞ yd Accent Fabric Cut (7) 4" Strips
Backing	⅔ yd Cut (2) 19" x 21" Pieces
Batting	20" x 34"

Cutting Techniques

Beginner's Cutting Kit

The proper tools are essential for your quilting
success. A large size rotary cutter, a 6" x 24" ruler,
and an 18" x 24" cutting mat are the "must-
haves" for beginning quilters. The Fiskars rotary
cutter is ergonomically contoured to fit your hand and
will lessen fatigue when cutting large amounts of strips.
When using a rotary cutter, you must use a cutting mat to
protect your blade and the surface below. A gridded cutting
mat is especially helpful in cutting straight and accurate strips.
Work in an area large enough so that fabric or strips never hang over
the edge of the table.

Quilt in a Day® Rulers

Quilt in a Day carries a wide selection of rulers for all your quilting needs. Besides the
6"x 24" ruler, it is helpful to have a 6" x 6" and a 16" Square Up when making the Log
Cabin quilt. Use a 6" x 6" square ruler for cutting 2½" center squares and conveniently
cutting blocks apart after you assembly-line sew. Use a 16" Square Up to square up your
finished blocks and the corners of your quilt.

Fiskars Craft Cutter

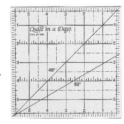

A combination ruler and cutting tool, the Craft
Cutter is very helpful for beginning quilters. The tool
is also especially helpful for anyone lacking strength due to
arthritis or Parkinson's disease. The ruler has an adhesive strip so it doesn't
slide easily. The cutting blade is attached to the ruler, so the cutter cannot 'stray'
from the ruler's edge. Placing a strip of adhesive tape or static tape along the 2½" line will
increase visibility and make cutting your Log Cabin strips even easier.

1. Cut a nick in one selvage, the tightly woven edge on both sides of the fabric. Tear across the grain from selvage to selvage.

2. Press the fabric, particularly the torn edge.

3. Fold the fabric in half, matching the frayed edges. Don't worry about the selvages not lining up correctly as this is not always possible. Line up the straight of the grain.

4. Place the fabric on the gridded mat with the folded edge along a horizontal line, and the torn edge on a vertical line.

5. Place the quarter inch line of the ruler along the torn edge of the fabric.

6. Spread your fingers and place four on top of the ruler with the little finger on the edge to keep the ruler firmly in place.

7. Take the rotary cutter in your free hand and open the blade. Starting below the fabric, begin cutting away from you, applying pressure on the ruler and the cutter. Keep the blade next to the ruler's edge.

8. **Cut strips for the blocks 2½" wide.** To help you, place an adhesive strip along the 2½" line on your ruler. Open the first strip and look at the fold to see if it is straight. If it has a crook that looks like an elbow, the fabric may not be folded on the straight of the grain. If this happens repeat the preceding steps.

9. **Borders are cut at different widths.** Check your particular yardage chart for measurements. Suggested widths to cut the border strips are given, but can be changed as long as you get the size quilt you desire. Some fabrics may not look attractive in the widths suggested. Fold the fabric to the finished size and lay them together with the quilt top before cutting all the strips.

If you are right-handed the fabric should trail off to the right.

The blade can be switched for left or right handed cutters.

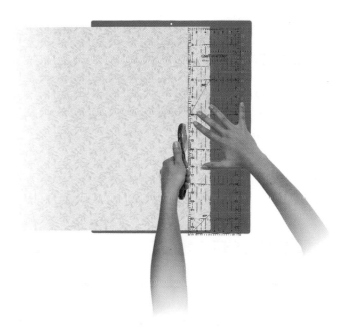

If you are left-handed the fabric should trail off to the left.

Sewing the Blocks

Sewing Techniques

Use a fine, sharp, #70/10 needle. Use small stitches, approximately 15 per inch, or 2.0 on computer machines with stitch selections from 1 to 4. Use a machine quilting needle and 10 stitches per inch, or 3.5 on a computer machine when sewing through batting.

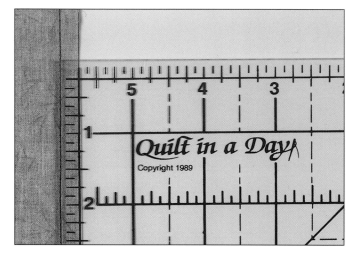

1/4" Seam Allowance

Sew an accurate and consistent ¼" seam allowance throughout the sewing of the quilt. Do not change machines in the middle of making the quilt. The width of the presser foot usually determines the seam allowance. If the measurement is less than ¼", place the guide at a slight distance from the presser foot for a consistent seam. Line the edges of the fabric with the edge of the presser foot and sew a few stitches. Measure the seam allowance. Use one of these tools to achieve a perfect ¼" seam allowance.

Magnetic Seam Guide

Placed directly on your sewing machine, the magnetic seam guide can be a great help in ensuring perfect ¼" seams for all your blocks. You may also use a strip of white adhesive tape or moleskin for this same purpose.

Sew Perfect Adhesive Seam Guide and Gauge

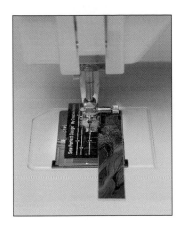

This is a plastic gauge with a hole located at the ¼" measurement along with an adhesive seam guide. Lower the needle into the ¼" mark, and align the left edge of the adhesive strip to the right side of the gauge. Press adhesive strip firmly into place.

1/4" Foot

Available for most sewing machines, a ¼" foot has a guide on it to help you keep your fabric from straying, giving you perfect ¼" seams. Your patchwork is then consistently accurate.

Neutral Thread

Sew the quilt blocks together with a good quality of neutral shade polyester or cotton spun thread. When machine quilting, use the same color thread as the backing in the bobbin. Heavy quilting thread is for hand quilting.

Using a Serger

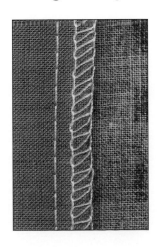

The Log Cabin is even quicker when sewn on a serger. A five thread serger with a chain stitch and an overcast stitch is best. If available, use the serger's fabric guide attachment, and make your seam adjustment by moving the guide. Do not let the serger's knife trim the edges. If a guide attachment is not available, stick a piece of moleskin to the serger so the seam is a ¼".

Fold and arrange the strips you prepared in the following order to the immediate right of your sewing
machine. Notice that they are not in the same order
as the Yardage and Cutting charts. This order is the
sewing order. Each fabric is used twice except for
the Center fabric.

The finished Log Cabin Block

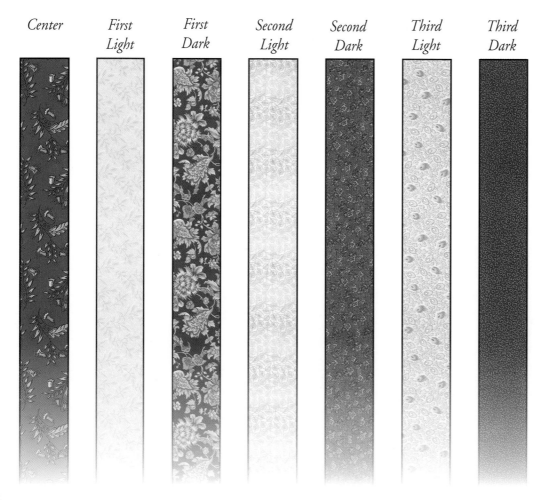

| Center | First Light | First Dark | Second Light | Second Dark | Third Light | Third Dark |

Making the Center Squares for the Entire Quilt

1. Take the Center strip and First Light strip. Place right sides together with the First Light on the bottom.

2. Sew the two strips together the whole length. Use a ¼" seam allowance and 15 stitches to the inch or 2.0 on computerized sewing machines. Sew additional strips for quilts larger than twin size.

Center   *First Light*

3. Place sewn strips straight on gridded cutting mat.

4. Trim left selvage edge straight with a rotary cutter and 6" x 6" ruler.

5. Cut into 2½" squares.

You should get approximately 17 squares from one strip.

Cut this many squares for your size quilt:

Center Square Chart			
Baby	9	Extra Long Double	24
Lap	12	Queen	24
Wallhanging	16	Square Queen	36
Regular Twin	15	King One	25
Extra Long Twin	18	King Two	36
Regular Double	20		

6. Center square fabric is used only once in the block. Remove left-over Center Square fabric from sewing area.

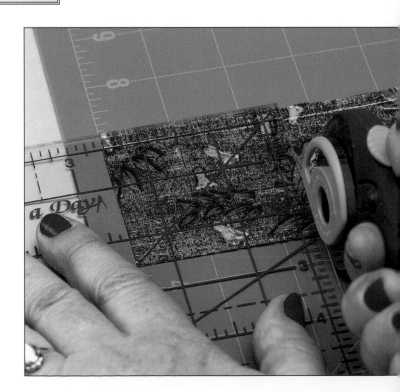

Adding Another First Light

Every fabric except Center is used twice in block. New strip always goes down first with right side up.

1. Turn stack over so the First Light is on the top. Line up stitching parallel with table. Think of the strip on the top as the "handle." This piece is always picked up at the top right corner, opened, and placed right sides together to the next strip.

2. Take a strip of First Light fabric. Place under presser foot with right side up.

3. Take a 2½" square, open, and place right sides together on the strip. Begin stitching down the right edge.

4. Stop and pull block so there are no puckers or tucks at seam. At seam, finger press both raw edges upward, or use your stiletto. Hold seam flat as you stitch over it.

5. As you near the end of the block, pick up the second block and open. Butt the second block right behind the first block. Sew through as before.

6. Continue in this order down the strip, butting and stitching, until you run out of strip. If there is not enough strip to fit an additional block, cut this waste off, and start with another strip and block.

"Handle"

If necessary, make second cut to trim excess.

7. Lay the strip straight on the cutting mat, with the block side up. Smooth. Line the ruler straight with the strip and the right edge of the block.

8. **Make one perpendicular cut** between blocks with the rotary cutter and ruler.

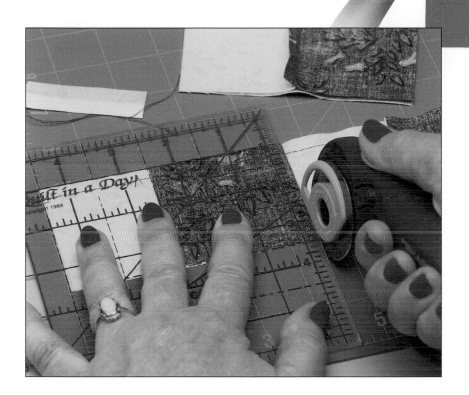

9. Stack. Turn stack over so the strip you just added is on the top. This top strip is your "handle" or the strip that goes to the top in the next step. Turn stack so stitching is parallel with table.

10. You no longer need the First Light strips. Remove the extra First Light strips from the immediate sewing area.

Adding First Dark Fabric

1. Take the First Dark strip. Place under presser foot with the right side up. Take the partially completed block, open, and place it right sides together to the strip.

Check block placement. The last color you added on must be to the top and perpendicular to the strip. In this case, it is the light color without the seam in it.

2. Stitch down the length of the block, pressing the seam up and flat with your stiletto. Make sure there are no puckers at the seams.

3. Butt on the next block, and maintain the same order. Continue until you have sewn a First Dark strip on all of your blocks.

Anticipate the last block. You should be able to sew nine blocks onto one strip. Cut off and discard the unusable part of the strip.

4. Cut apart between blocks with the cutter and ruler. Make sure each cut is perpendicular with the top of the strip.

5. Stack. Turn stack over. Line up stack so stitches are parallel with table.

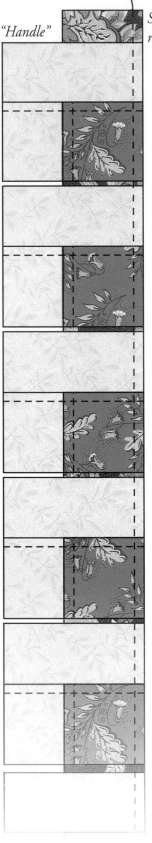

"Handle" *Strip down first right side up*

Adding Another First Dark Fabric

1. Place another First Dark strip under presser foot with right side up. Place the blocks right sides together to the strip. The last color added must be on the top and perpendicular to the strip. In this case, it is a First Dark strip.

2. Stitch down the length of the block, pushing the first seam up and flat, and the second seam down and flat.

3. Butt on the next block.

4. Continue stitching down the length of the strip, butting on blocks and new strips as necessary until you have completed your total number of blocks.

Remember to anticipate the ends of your strips. You should be able to sew about six blocks onto a strip at this step. Discard the few inches at the bottom.

5. Cut the blocks apart. Stack. Turn stack over.

6. You will no longer need the First Dark fabric. Remove extra First Dark strips from the immediate sewing area.

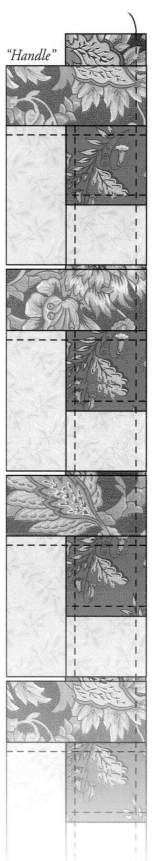

"Handle"

The first seam is sewn up

The second seam is sewn down

Repeat as above

Adding the Second Light

1. Place a Second Light strip under presser foot with right side up. Place a block right sides together to the strip.

The First Dark, which is last color you added, will be on the top and perpendicular to the new strip.

2. Stitch down the blocks, sewing the first seams up and the second seams down.

3. You should be able to sew six blocks on each strip at this point. Anticipate the ends and discard the few inches of waste.

4. Cut the blocks apart. Stack. Turn stack over.

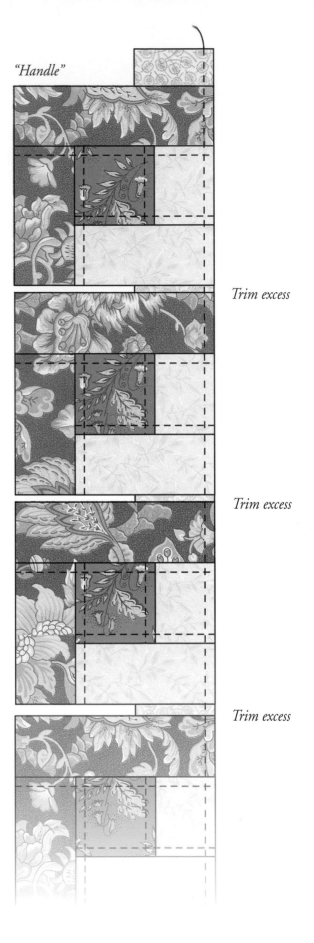

"Handle"

Trim excess

Trim excess

Trim excess

Adding Another Second Light

At this point you should have as many blocks as your finished quilt should have, and the backs of those partially completed blocks should appear something like the illustration to the right. Work in a rotating motion. The light colors line up beside the lights; the darks line up beside the other darks.

1. Repeat, adding another Second Light to all of your blocks as before. This step yields five blocks per strip.

2. Cut the blocks apart. Stack. Turn stack over.

"Handle"

Adding the Second Dark

1. Place a Second Dark strip under presser foot with right side up. Place a block right sides together to the strip.

The Second Light, which is last color you added, will be on the top and perpendicular to the new strip.

2. Stitch down the blocks, sewing the first seams up and the second seams down.

3. You should be able to sew five blocks on each strip at this point. Anticipate the ends and discard the few inches of waste.

4. Cut the blocks apart. Stack. Turn stack over.

"Handle"

Adding Another Second Dark

Work in a rotating motion. The light colors line up beside the lights; the darks line up beside the other darks.

1. Add another Second Dark to all of your blocks. This step yields four blocks per strip.

2. Cut the blocks apart. Stack. Turn stack over.

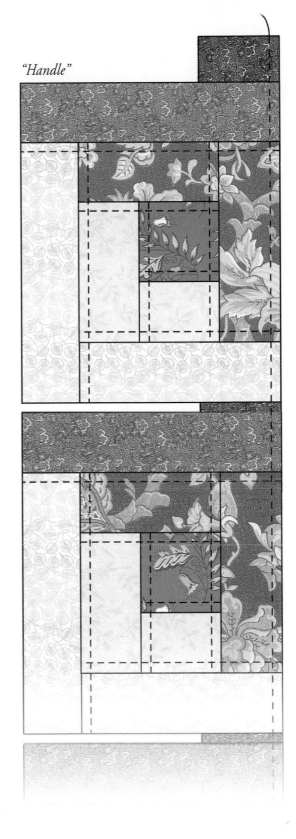

"Handle"

Adding the Third Light

1. Place a Third Light strip under presser foot with right side up. Place a block right sides together to the strip.

The Second Dark, which is last color you added, will be on the top and perpendicular to the new strip.

2. Stitch down the blocks, sewing the first seams up and the second seams down.

3. You should be able to sew four blocks on each strip at this point. Anticipate the ends.

4. Cut the blocks apart. Stack. Turn stack over.

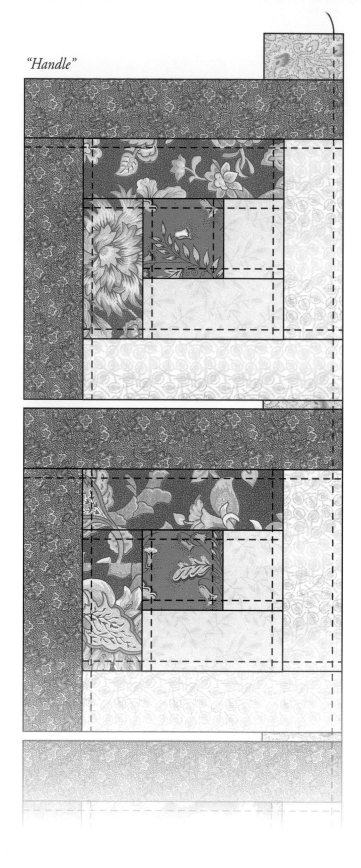

"Handle"

44

Adding Another Third Light

Work in a rotating motion. The light colors line up beside the lights; the darks line up beside the other darks.

1. Add another Third Light to all of your blocks. This step yields three blocks per strip.

2. Cut the blocks apart. Stack. Turn stack over.

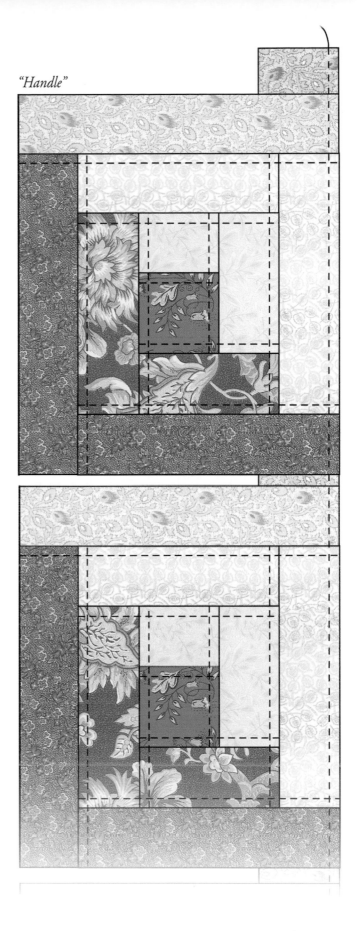

"Handle"

Adding the Third Dark

1. Place a Third Dark strip under presser foot with right side up. Place a block right sides together to the strip.

The Third Light, which is last color you added, will be on the top and perpendicular to the new strip.

2. Stitch down the blocks, sewing the first seams up and the second seams down.

3. You should be able to sew three blocks on each strip at this point.

4. Cut the blocks apart. Stack. Turn stack over.

"Handle"

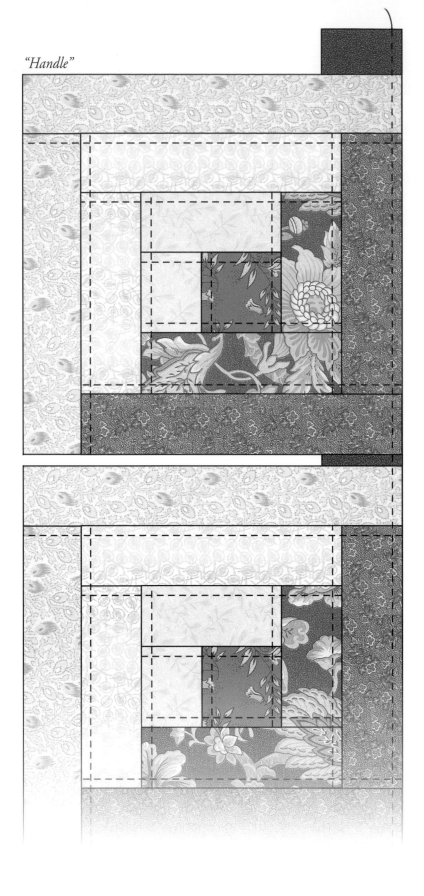

Adding Another Third Dark

Work in a rotating motion. The light colors line up beside the lights; the darks line up beside the other darks.

1. Add another Third Dark to all of your blocks. This step yields three blocks per strip.

2. Cut the blocks apart. Stack. Turn stack over.

"Handle"

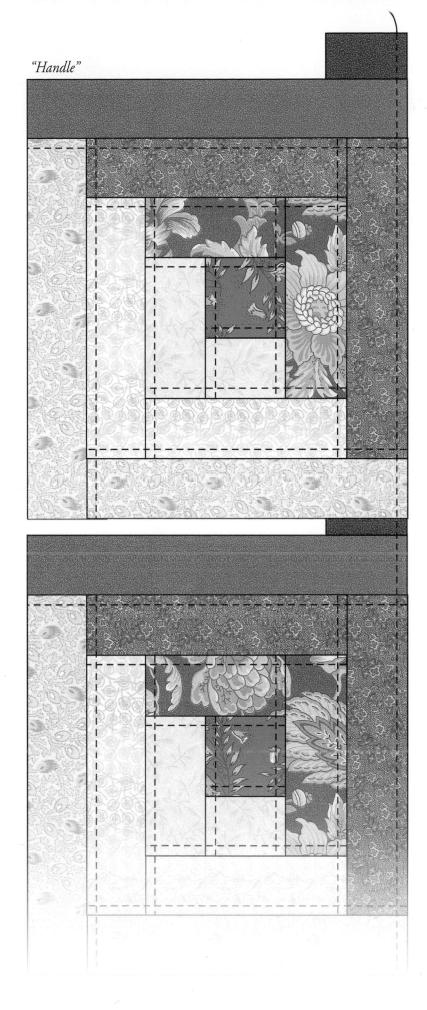

Pressing and Squaring Up the Finished Block

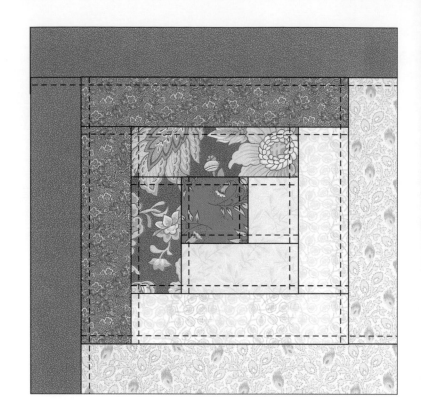

Seams on the finished block should lay flat from the center out. If any seams are turned in the wrong direction, it's best to just leave them as they are, or re-sew that particular seam. Clipping the seam would weaken it and eventually a hole would result.

Pressing

1. Place the block on gridded pressing mat.

2. Carefully press the blocks from the right side. Keep square on the pressing mat.

3. Press the blocks from the wrong side. All seams should lay flat from the center out.

4. As you press, check for edges that need to be trimmed.

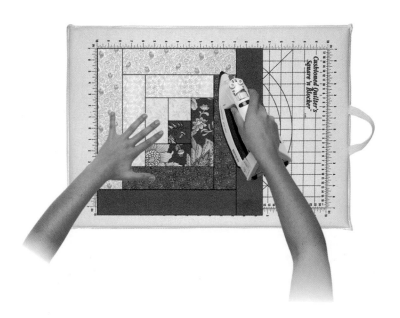

Squaring Up

Log Cabin blocks are very "forgiving" if they are not perfectly square. They stretch easily when sewing them into a finished top. For this reason, it may not be necessary to square up your blocks.

1. Place blocks on top of each other to see if they are approximately the same size.

2. Set aside any blocks that are approximately ¾" larger.

3. Sliver trim the larger blocks equally on four sides to the average size.

   ■ Place diagonal line of the 16" Square Up ruler across the center of the block.

   ■ Trim on two sides.

   ■ Turn, and trim equal amounts on the remaining two sides.

4. Re-press blocks that are smaller than the average block. When the top is sewn together, stretch these to fit the others, or use a skimpy seam allowance on that block. Reinforce the skimpy seam.

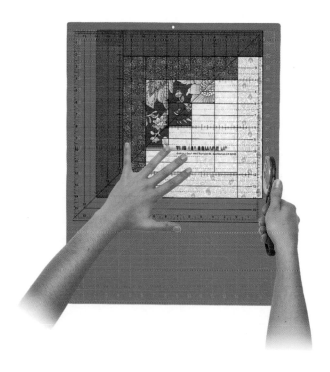

Previewing the Quilt Top

Lay out your completed blocks on your bed or on the floor so that you can choose your design. Quilt pattern layouts are on the following pages.

Size Chart	
9 Block Baby 52	24 Block Extra Long Double . . 56–57
12 Block Lap 53	24 Block Queen 56–57
16 Block Wallhanging 54–55	36 Block Square Queen 58–59
15 Block Regular Twin 53	25 Block King One 56
18 Block Extra Long Twin 52	36 Block King Two 58–59
20 Block Double 57	

Turn the blocks into the positions shown for your selected pattern. Use the Third Dark as your guide. If you are having trouble choosing a layout, you may find it helpful to take a polaroid photo of your blocks in each design you are considering.

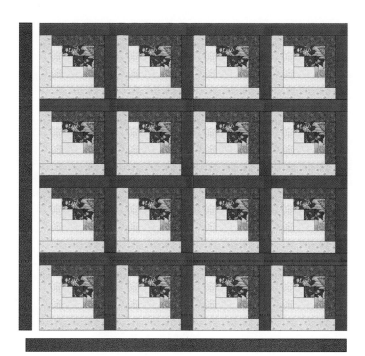

In the All Sevens layout, the pattern looks more complete if you sew extra Third Dark strips on the left and bottom sides after the quilt top is sewn together. All Sevens refers to the direction of the Third Dark.

Most blocks, regardless of color combination, look attractive in the Fields and Furrows layout. Think of the Third Darks as Sevens and L's.

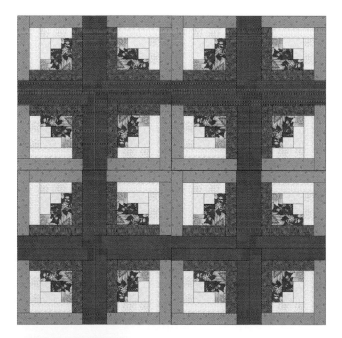

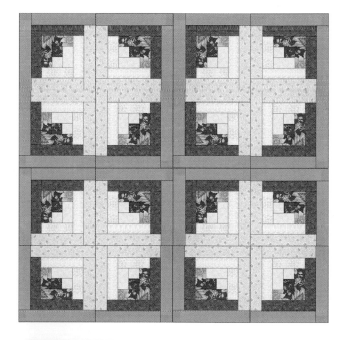

If the Third Light is much darker than the other two lights, and stands out considerably, try the Dark with Light pattern. The Third Light then appears as a frame.

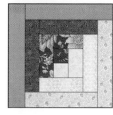

If the Third Dark fabric is different and stands out from the other fabrics, try the Light with Dark pattern.

18 Block Layouts   Extra Long Twin

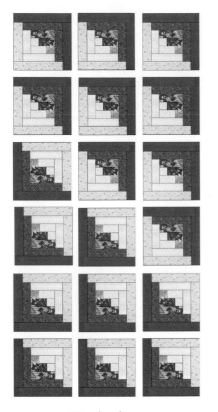

Timberline

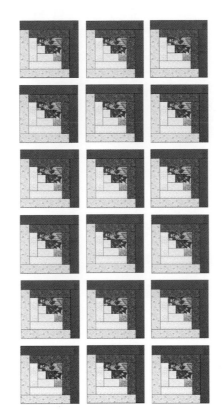

All Sevens

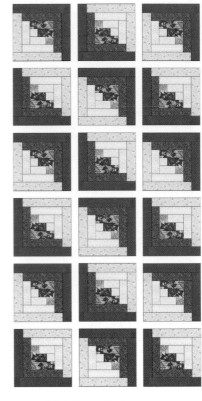

Fields and Furrows

9 Block Layouts   Baby

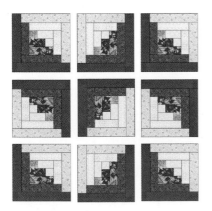

Zig Zag

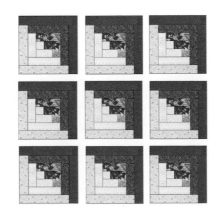

All Sevens

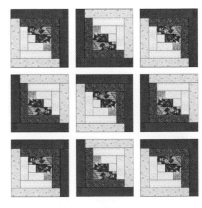

Fields and Furrows

15 Block Layouts   Regular Twin

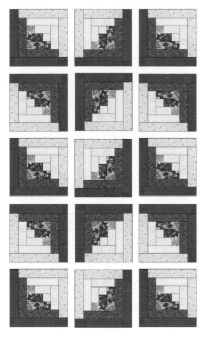

Zig Zag

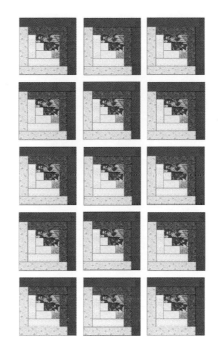

All Sevens

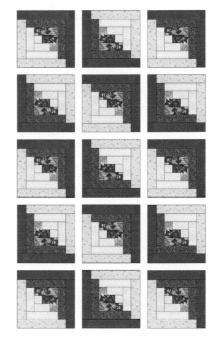

Fields and Furrows

12 Block Layouts   Lap

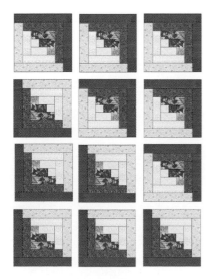

Timberline

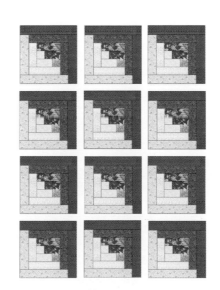

All Sevens

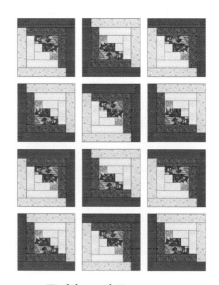

Fields and Furrows

Light with Dark

Navajo

Positive/Negative

Starlight

Fields and Furrows

Whirligig

Peaks and Valleys

All Sevens

Zig Zag

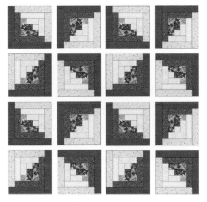

Windmill

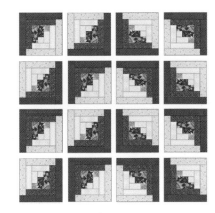

Arrow

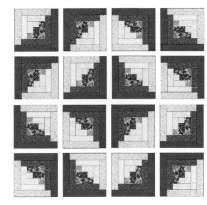

Barn Raising

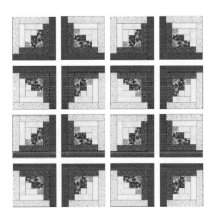

Dark with Light

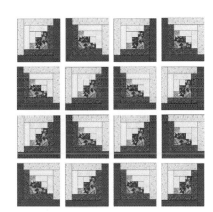

Mountains

25 Block Layouts King One

All Sevens

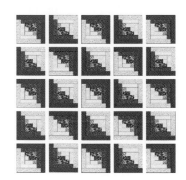

Fields and Furrows

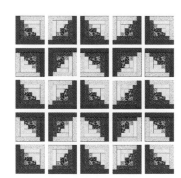

Zig Zag

24 Block Layouts Queen–Extra Long Double

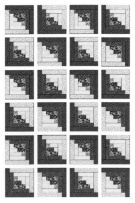

Fields and Furrows

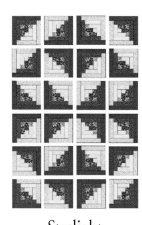

Starlight

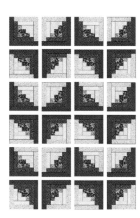

Zig Zag

All Sevens

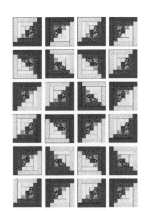

Whirligig

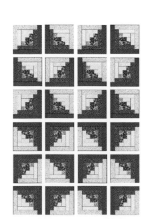

Peaks and Valleys

Four Square

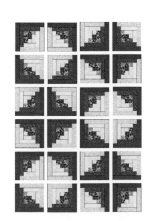

Positive/Negative

56

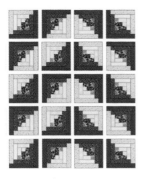

Arrows

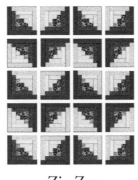

Zig Zag

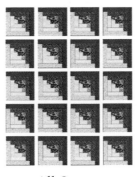

All Sevens

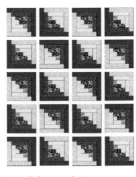

Fields and Furrows

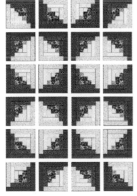

Cross Hatch

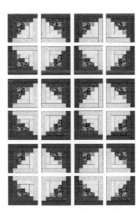

Light with Dark

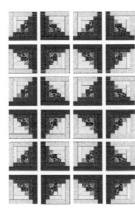

Dark with Light

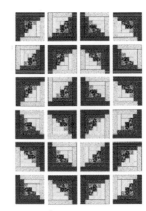

Barn Raising

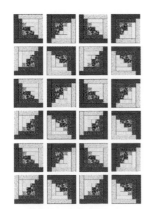

Windmill

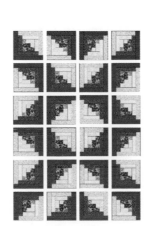

Navajo

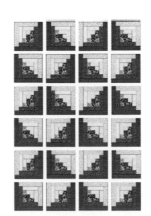

Mountains

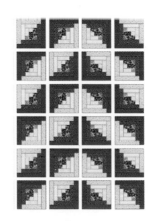

Arrow

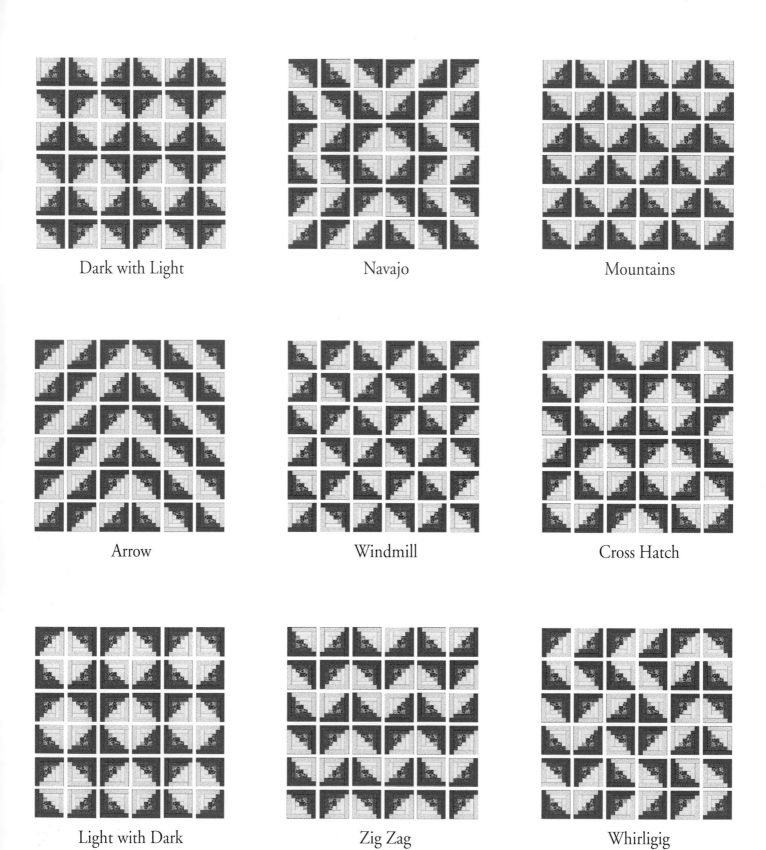

Dark with Light

Navajo

Mountains

Arrow

Windmill

Cross Hatch

Light with Dark

Zig Zag

Whirligig

Fields and Furrows

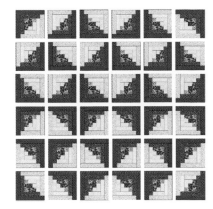

Peaks and Valleys

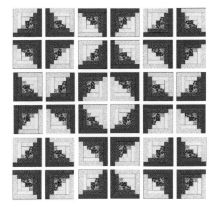

Stained Glass

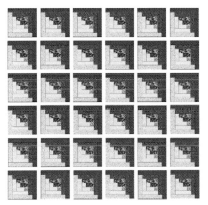

All Sevens

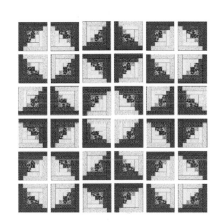

Positive/Negative

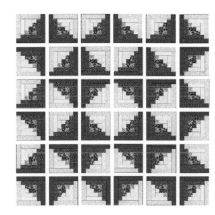

Four Square

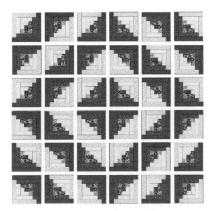

Barn Raising

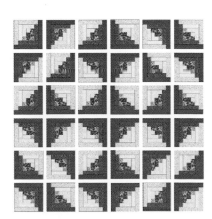

Starburst

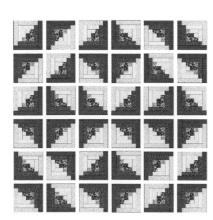

Starlight

Sewing the Quilt Top Together

Quilter's Straight Pins

Quilter's straight pins have a long shank and a bright yellow head for high visibility. Use straight pins to pin blocks together and to pin borders to your quilt top.

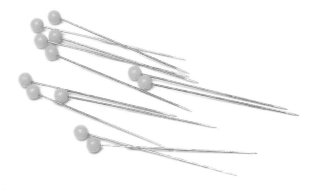

After the blocks are all laid out in your selected pattern, sew the top together in numbered order.

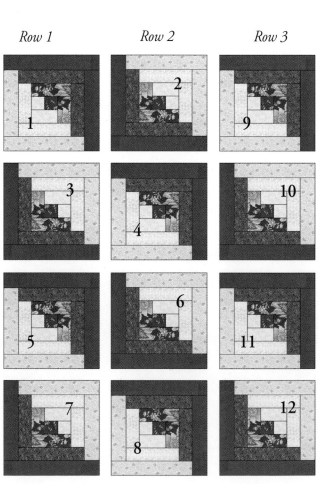

Example: Lap Robe in the Fields and Furrows pattern

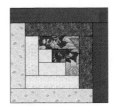
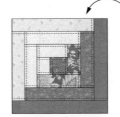

Sewing the First Two Vertical Rows

1. Flip the second row onto the first row right sides together.

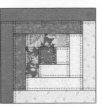

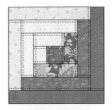

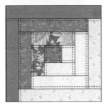

2. Starting at the top, pick up the blocks from top down, adding each new pair to the bottom of the pile so Blocks 1 and 2 are still on top. Take the stack of blocks to your sewing machine.

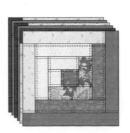

As you sew the top together, push seams on wrong side of block as pressed. On right sides, match seams across from each other.

Lock the outside edges. Finger pin opposite corner and stretch the two to meet.

3. Pick up Blocks 1 and 2. Open and check the block orientation against the layout chart. Flip right sides together.

4. Lock the outside edges. Stitch down about 1", maintaining a ¼" seam. This anchors the two together. Finger pin the other corner and stretch the two to meet. Stitch. Do not cut the threads.

5. Pick up Blocks 3 and 4. Open and check their orientation. Flip them right sides together. Assembly-line sew Blocks 3 and 4 after the first two.

6. Anchor the two with 1" of stitching. Finger pin the corners as before. Stretch the two to meet. Stitch.

7. Continue assembly-line sewing the blocks together in the first two vertical rows. Backstitch. **Do not clip the connecting threads.**

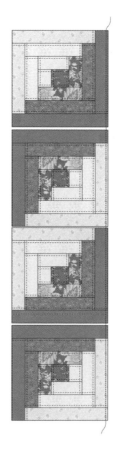

Sewing the Third Vertical Row

1. Open Rows 1 and 2. Place beside the blocks in vertical Row 3.

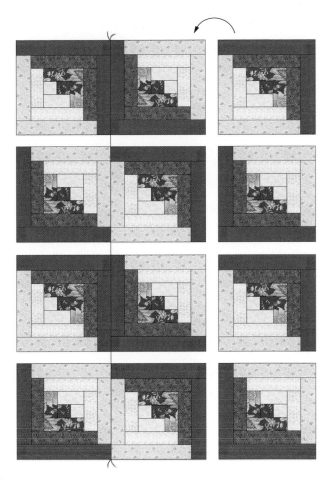

2. Pick up the first block in vertical Row 3, and flip right sides together to Block 2. Pin the outside edges of the blocks together.

3. Flip the next block of vertical Row 3 right sides together to Block 4. Pin the outside edges together.

4. Continue in this manner down the third vertical row until all of the blocks are pinned in place.

5. **Overlap** and pin the corners of the blocks together, so when you pick up the top, the blocks are pinned in a chain.

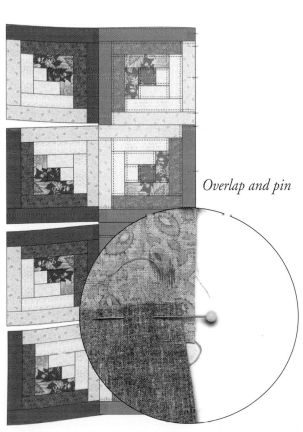

Overlap and pin

6. Sew the third vertical row to the first two vertical rows.

7. Continue pinning and sewing all the vertical rows until all of the blocks are sewn together. **Do not clip the connecting threads.**

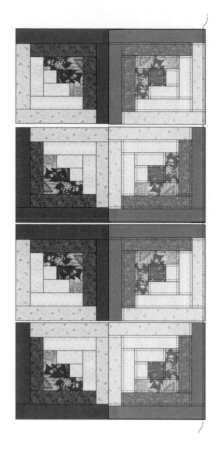

The illustration shows a 12 block quilt as it looks after the vertical rows are sewn. Assembly-line sewing, without cutting connecting threads, makes the remaining steps much easier. The connecting threads are equal to pin matching.

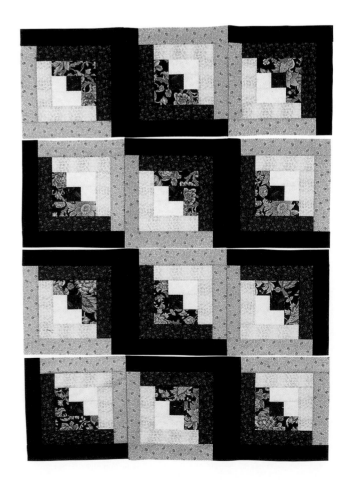

Sewing the Horizontal Rows Together

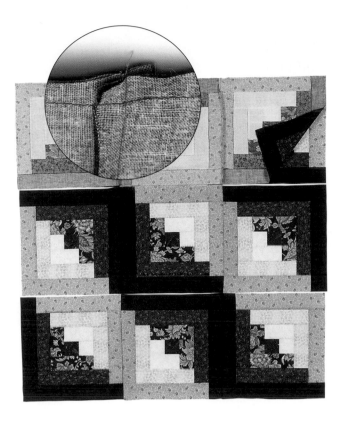

1. Flip the top horizontal row down on the second horizontal row, with right sides together.

2. Backstitch at the beginning and end of the row. Stretch and stitch the blocks to meet.

3. At the connecting thread, push the top seam up and the bottom seam down. As you sew the horizontal rows, check the direction those seams were pressed on the opposite side of the block, and finger press in that direction so seams do not twist.

4. Complete all horizontal rows in the same manner, keeping the last sewn row on top to check direction of seams.

5. Press top from wrong and right side.

Borders & Backing

Borders

Refer to your Yardage Chart for the various widths. Border widths are merely suggestions depending on your fabric. A narrower or wider border may be more attractive. All are cut selvage to selvage, and are approximately 42" long.

You need two strips longer than the length of the quilt, and two strips longer than the width of the quilt for each fabric.

The borders are generally added in a narrow to wide order. The illustration at the right shows the numbered order in which the strips are added.

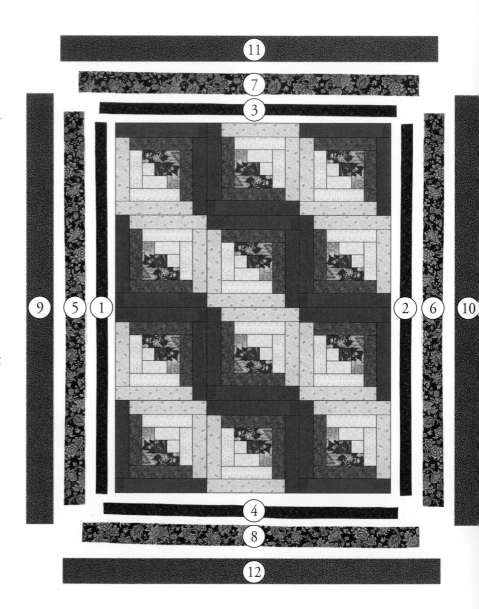

Adding the Borders

1. Straighten the ends of border strips and remove selvages with rotary cutter and ruler.

2. Measure the length of the quilt down the center and both sides. If the measurements differ, take an average.

3. Sew sets of strips together to make two strips longer than the length.

You may not need to piece the First Border strips for the Baby Quilt. Lap Robes may need only 1½ strips sewn together. You may need to sew up to three strips together for the King size quilts.

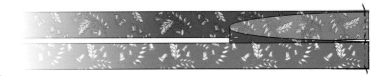

4. Cut the strips to that measurement for both long sides.

5. Find the mid-point of the strip and pin to the mid-point of the sides of the quilt. Pin at both ends and between every three inches.

You may center your seams on the right side of the quilt if you wish. It is, however, difficult to detect a seam in a printed fabric, and less noticeable if seams are randomly placed.

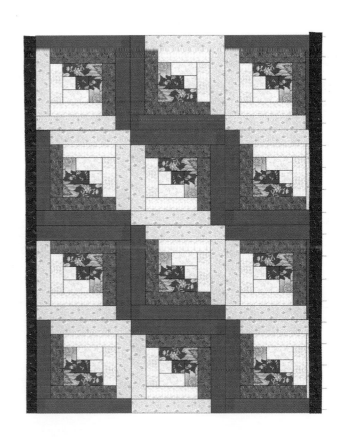

6. Sew with a ¼" seam allowance, stretching or easing as necessary.

7. Repeat on the opposite side.

8. Set the seams, open, and press seam allowances toward the border.

9. Measure the width of the quilt across the center, top and bottom including the side borders. If the measurements differ, take an average.

10. Sew two sets of strips together for larger quilts.

11. Cut the strips to that measurement for the top and bottom edges.

12. Find the mid-point of the strips and pin to the mid-point of the top and bottom edge. Pin at both ends and between every three inches.

13. Sew with a ¼" seam allowance, stretching or easing as necessary. Repeat on the opposite side.

14 . Set the seam, and press seam allowances toward the border.

Repeat this method for additional borders.

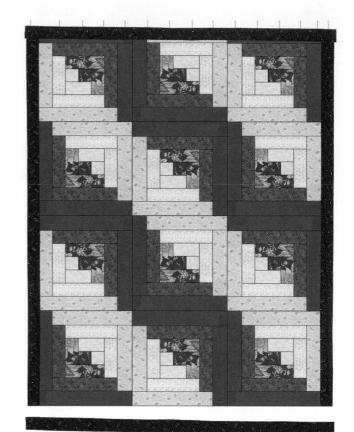

Preparing the Backing

If you are using 42" wide yardage for your backing, divide the fabric into two or three equal lengths, depending on the width of your quilt. Refer to your yardage charts.

1. Cut a nick next to one selvage and tear away selvage edges. Press.

2. Place the torn edges right sides together. Pin and sew a ½" seam allowance.

3. Repeat for additional backing pieces if needed.

4. Press the seam allowance to one side.

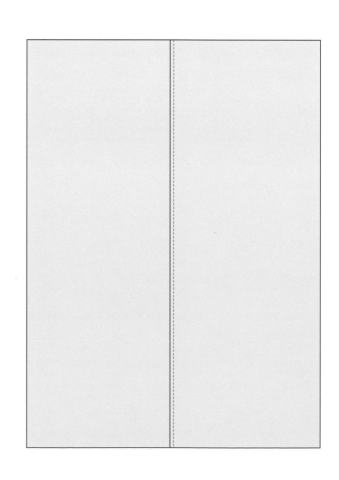

Choosing How to Finish Your Quilt

There are two different methods described for finishing your quilt: the Quick Turn and Tie Method and the Machine Quilt and Bind Method. Each one has advantages and disadvantages, and each requires a different sewing skill level.

Quick Turn and Tie Method

The Quick Turn and Tie Method is the easiest and fastest method of finishing the quilt. The backing and quilt top are sewn right sides together, and the batting is then rolled into the middle of the quilt, just before tying. Binding is not necessary with this technique.

If you wish to put thick batting in your quilt and your machine has a difficult time sewing through it, this is a good method to use. Tying all three layers together eliminates the need for machine sewing through all thicknesses. If you use thin batting, you can machine stitch through the borders once the batting is turned into the middle. You need a sturdy machine to sew through three layers of fabric and batting, plus a large table or floor area to work on.

Machine Quilt and Bind Method

Quilts finished with this method look more like "antique quilts," although it requires more time and skill. The backing, batting, and quilt top are layered and safety pinned together. Quilting lines are marked or eyeballed later while quilting. You need to have a large table to layer and pin. A walking foot is necessary to avoid puckers on the back side. After quilting, a straight grain strip of binding is added to the outside edge. If you use 100% cotton batting, you can give the quilt an old finished look by laundering and drying it upon completion.

There are other options if you choose not to finish your quilt yourself. You can send the top out to a service that does quilting with a professional machine or to a professional hand quilter.

Machine Quilting By a Professional Service

A professional using a hand guided quilting machine can add a special touch to your handmade treasure. Here are some things to remember when taking your quilt to a professional quilting service: your quilt top must be squared and pressed, free of loose threads, and clean. All seams must be secure. Take them a good quality batting such as Hobbs, Warm & Natural, Thermolam, or Hobbs Heirloom Cotton. The batting and backing *must* be two inches larger than the quilt on all sides. Layers must be separate, not pinned or basted together. (Each layer goes into the machine separately.) The backing must be squared and pressed. If a colored thread is to be used on the top, matching thread goes in the bobbin. If invisible thread is used on top, thread to match the backing color will be used in the bobbin. If 100% cotton thread is used, all fabrics in your quilt must be prewashed. Some also offer metallic or multicolored threads. You can find a service of this type through your local quilt shop or guild, or through advertisements in quilt magazines. The cost is minimal compared to the beautiful results.

Hand Quilting by a Professional Group

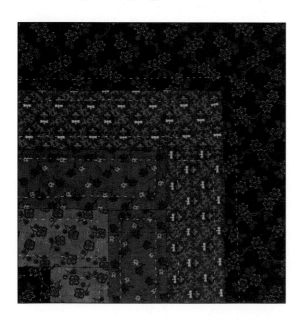

Hand quilting gives your quilt the traditional look. This method is best used to add heirloom quality to a quilt which is not for everyday use, but will be passed on in the family. Quilt guilds and church groups sometimes accept projects for hand quilting, although there may be a waiting list. Church members donate their time and put the fee back into the church or a service project. Check with the group to find out their requirements for backing and batting. The cost is higher because of the labor involved. Also, be aware that there may be some variations in stitching, due to the fact that several people work on each quilt. Some individuals hand quilt for a living. Look for their advertisements in quilt magazines.

Products

Binder Clamps

Large three inch binder clamps are available at office supply stores. Use binder clamps to secure and smooth backing to table for pinning. You do need strength in your hands to open them, but they will clamp onto tables 1" thick. If binder clamps are not available, use two inch wide industrial strength tape to secure the quilt back to a table.

Basting Clamps

Basting clamps, made of white pvc plastic, are also designed to secure batting and backing to the table for pinning. They require little strength to manipulate, and easily wrap around the edges of six to eight foot work tables with folding legs.

Safety Pins

If you plan to machine quilt your Log Cabin, nickel-plated safety pins in the one inch size are best for basting quilt layers together. They are small enough to prevent the layers from moving as you machine quilt, and they are rust resistant.

Kwik Klip™

The Kwik Klip™ is a tool used to open and close safety pins. The Kwik Klip™ fits into the hand and has a ribbed tip that catches the safety pin for easy closure. After the safety pin has been inserted into the quilt layers, use the tool to guide the safety pin closed. It can also be used to open closed safety pins.

Curved Needle and Embroidery Floss

Use all six strands of embroidery floss or crochet thread to tie the three layers together. Use wool yarn if you are interested in a bolder look. Use a fine curved needle with a large eye for drawing the yarn through the fabrics. A pair of pliers to pull the needle through makes the job much easier.

Hera Marker

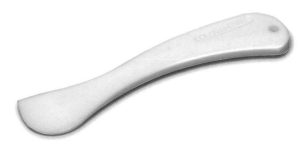

The Hera Marker is a plastic tool with a sharp edge used to press in the lines to be quilted. It is held in much the same way as a rotary cutter with a ruler. Line up the marker with the ruler and push the tool away from you. The marker creases the fabric as you push, leaving a non-permanent line.

Invisible Thread

If you're machine quilting for the first time, your stitch length and accuracy will not be perfect. Invisible thread helps hide some of the imperfections. Another advantage to using invisible thread is that you don't need to change thread color as you stitch over various colored fabrics. Choose smoky-colored for dark fabrics or clear for a range of colors from white to dark. Use invisible thread in the needle and regular thread to match the backing in the bobbin case. Reduce the upper tension on your sewing machine to make a balanced stitch.

Walking Foot

The walking foot is an attachment that has teeth similar to those on the feed dogs. When you have several layers of fabric to sew, these teeth propel the fabric layers at the same pace, which helps to eliminate puckers on the front and back of the quilt. Use the walking foot for straight line stitching methods such as "stitch in the ditch."

Jaws™

Jaws™, made of flexible Lexon®, are open rings with grips to wrap around part of a quilt and hold it tight while machine quilting the rest of the quilt. They come in two sizes; the smaller size is perfect for smaller quilts. You can also wrap and hold the excess off the floor while quilting.

Quick Turn and Tie Method

1. Clamp or tape the backing **right side up** to a large surface, as a ping pong table, or dining room table. Smooth it, but don't pull it taut. You can also tape the backing to a hard floor, or pin backing to a plush carpet by pushing straight pins through the fabric.

2. Center the quilt top, wrong side up, on the backing. Leave a couple of inches of backing showing on all sides. Smooth from the center out.

3. Pin close to the edge around the border, but leave an opening in the center of the long side. The batting, backing, and top will be turned through this opening.

The size of the opening will depend on the size of your quilt and the thickness or loft of batting you choose. Leave a 24" opening for large quilts and/or high lofts and 18" for smaller quilts and/or low lofts.

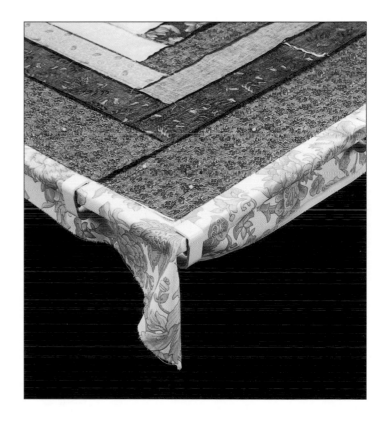

4. Make a cross with two pins at the beginning, and at the end of the opening. Do not sew in this space.

5. Begin sewing a ¼" seam at the crossed pins. Do not backstitch because when quick-turning, you want the stitching to "give" instead of tearing the fabric.

6. Sew all around until you reach the other crossed pins. Do not backstitch.

7. Trim backing to the edges of the quilt.

8. Follow the package instructions to relax batting prior to using.

9. Lay the batting on the large surface. Do not stretch the batting. Smooth out any bumps or creases. Clamp or tape to surface. Lay the quilt top/backing on the batting with the wrong side of the blocks showing. Leave a couple of inches of batting showing on all sides. Smooth out with a yard stick.

10. Hand baste a running stitch through all layers around the edge in the seam allowance. At the opening, baste only the backing to the batting to make the opening easier to sew closed.

11. Trim away batting to the edges of the quilt.

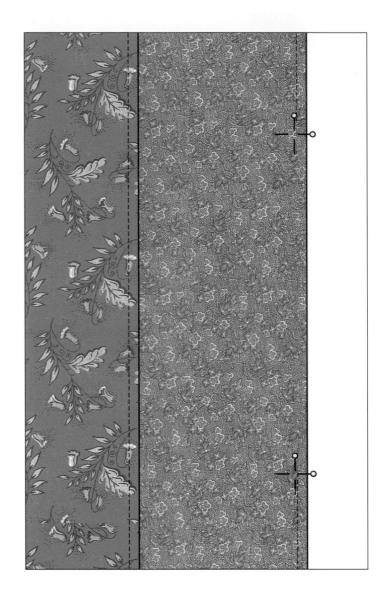

Quick Turning

1. Gather four friends or family to the corners of the quilt. Gather more if it is a large one.

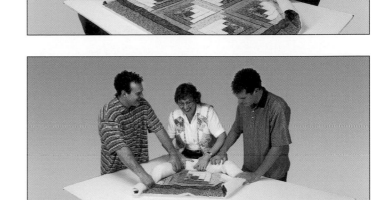

2. Roll toward the opening.

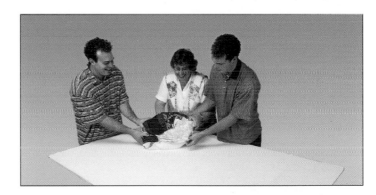

3. Fold the top layer of the opening back and gently pull out the quilt, turning it right side out.

4. Unroll the quilt.

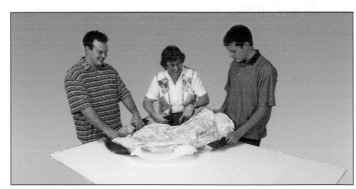

5. Holding the edges tightly, pull from opposite sides to position the batting. Stretch and shake it to remove lumps and bumps. Turn it over and do the same.

6. Pick out the corners with a large needle or stiletto.

Closing the Opening

1. In the middle of the opening, fold under the raw edge of the quilt ¼". Match to the raw edge of the backing and pin. Repeat on both sides until opening is pinned closed.

2. Thread a hand sewing needle with a double strand of thread and knot.

3. Take a stitch in the seam allowance through the opening to bury the knot. Bring the needle out through the lining fold and take a stitch in the backing just across from that stitch. Repeat, working your way along the opening until it is completely closed.

4. Take a few back stitches, knot, and clip the threads.

Squaring the Corners of the Quilt

1. Lay the quilt on a flat surface. Make sure the blocks and borders are straight in all directions.

2. Place the 16" Square Up ruler on a corner block. Push and smooth the quilt top until the seams line up with the outside edges of the ruler. Safety pin through all layers in the First Border.

3. Repeat on all borders on all corners.

Safety Pinning

Grasp the opened pin in your right hand and the Kwik Klip™ in your left hand. Push the pin through the three layers, take a ½" bite, and bring the tip of the pin back out. Catch the tip in the groove of the Kwik Klip™. Push pin closed.

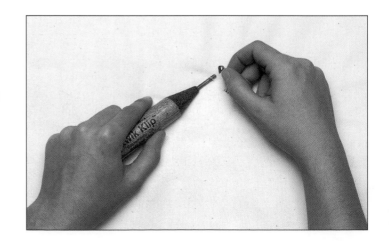

Tying

You may tie down the whole quilt, or just the center of the quilt and "stitch in the ditch" around the borders. Enhance the quilt pattern with ties following the design. Place a cutting mat under the quilt as you pin and tie. Check your batting instructions to see how close together you should tie. Tie at least in the center and corner of every block, and 6" apart on the borders.

1. Put a straight pin at each place you plan to tie.

2. Thread a large-eyed curved needle with about two yards of all six strands of embroidery floss. Wind the extra floss on an empty spool to keep it from knotting.

3. Place the needle point behind a pin. When the needle strikes the mat, bend your hand back and the point of the needle will wrap itself around the pin. With a finger of the opposite hand, control the size of the "bite." Pull the needle through, leaving two inches of floss for tying.

4. Draw the needle and floss along to each point, stitching in and out, and replacing the tying material as you need it.

5. Clip all the stitches midway.

6. Cross the strands of floss. Take the top strand and loop it around and under the other strand twice. (See Black.) Pull the strands in opposite directions as in tying a shoelace.

7. Cross the strands of floss again, the opposite way that you crossed them before. Take the top strand and loop it around and under the other strand twice. (See White.) Pull the strands in opposite directions.

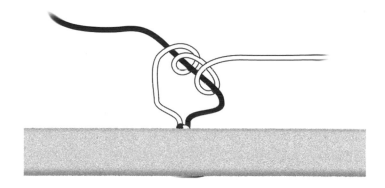

8. Cut the floss to your desired length, or approximately ½" long.

Stitching in the Ditch

"Stitching in the Ditch" is the term used for sewing in the depth of the seams, adding dimension to the borders.

1. Place a "walking foot" attachment on your sewing machine.

2. Use regular or invisible thread as a top thread. Match the bobbin thread to the backing fabric. Lengthen the stitch to 10 stitches per inch or 3.5 on computer machines. Test the stitching by sewing through two layers of fabric, and a batting scrap. Reduce the top tension if necessary.

3. Safety pin baste down the center of each border.

4. Position the quilt so it is not hanging off the end of the sewing table.

5. Place the needle in the depth of the First Border seam. Place your hands in a triangle shape. Backstitch or lock stitch. Sew forward. Stop and check for puckers. Sew to the end of the border, adjusting the quilt as necessary.

To avoid puckering on thick batting, run your right hand along the back, checking before you sew. With your left hand, stretch all layers away from you, and with your right hand, stretch all layers toward you while stitching.

6. Leave the needle in the quilt as you pivot to the next side. Continue stitching in the ditch around the First Border. Lock stitch or backstitch when you get back to where you started.

7. Stitch in the ditch through all borders in the same manner.

CHAPTER 12

Machine Quilt and Bind Method

1. Lay backing out flat on the floor or large table area with the right side down. A ping pong table makes a great working space. A block tile floor helps in squaring the quilt up. Clamp or tape.

2. Spread the bonded batting on top. Reclamp the batting with the backing.

3. Lay the quilt top right side up in the middle of the batting and backing. Check that you have at least 2" of batting and backing around the quilt top.

4. Carefully hand smooth from the center out to the corners and outer edges. Do not stretch.

5. Check to see that the borders and blocks are straight. Smooth and push them until they are straight lines.

6. Place the 16" Square Up ruler on a corner block. Push and smooth the First Border until the seams line up with the outside edges of the ruler. Safety pin through all layers in the First Border.

7. Repeat on all borders for all corners.

Planning and Marking the Quilting Lines

Plan where you will machine quilt. The quilting should enhance the pattern.

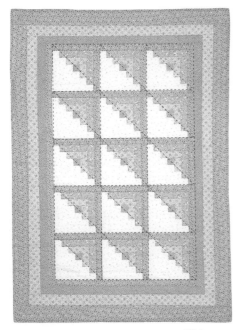

All Sevens

In a pattern such as All Sevens, quilt the straight lines "in the ditch" between rows to anchor the three layers together. In addition, quilt through all three layers on the diagonal.

Barn Raising

In a pattern such as Barn Raising, quilt a diamond shape from the center out.

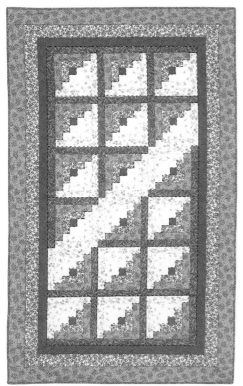

Timberline

In a pattern such as Timberline, quilt the straight lines between rows without stitching through the light band of fabric. Stairstep quilting is also effective. Use the needle down position on the sewing machine, sew "in the ditch" on each strip and pivot with the needle in the quilt.

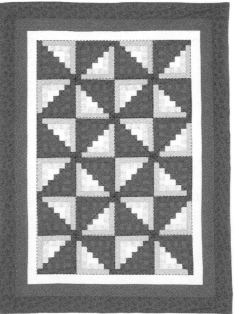

Windmill

In a pattern such as Windmill, quilt the straight lines in the ditch between rows to anchor the three layers together. Then quilt on the diagonals in both directions.

You can mark the quilting line now, or "eyeball" the lines later when machine quilting.

1. To mark now, place the 6" x 24" ruler on the planned quilting line. Line up a Hera marker against the edge of the ruler, and push the tool away from you. The marker creases the fabric as you push, leaving a non-permanent line.

2. Place safety pins away from the planned quilting lines. Flip the quilt over and check for puckering around the pins. If there is puckering, remove the pins, smooth, and pin again.

The fast and easy way to close and open safety pins is with a Kwik Klip™ pinning tool. In one hand hold the Kwik Klip™ and with the other hand hold a safety pin with the middle finger and thumb. Insert the point of the pin through all layers of the quilt, and taking a ½" bite, bring the point of the pin up through the quilt onto the Kwik Klip™ between the notches. Using the index finger, push the head of the pin down over the point to close it.

3. Remove clamps. Trim the batting and backing, leaving at least two inches beyond the quilt top.

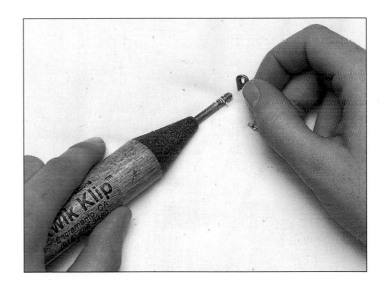

Machine Quilting

1. Place a "walking foot" attachment on your sewing machine.

2. Use regular or invisible thread as a top thread. Match the bobbin thread to the backing fabric. Lengthen the stitch to 10 stitches per inch, or setting 3.5 on computerized sewing machines. Test the stitching by sewing through two layers of fabric and a batting scrap. If the invisible thread puckers the quilt, reduce the top tension. If the walking foot drags on the quilt, reduce the foot pressure.

3. Roll the quilt from one side toward the middle if you are quilting in straight rows. Roll the quilt from one corner on the diagonal toward the middle if you are stairstep or diagonal line quilting.

4. Place Jaws™ around the rolled edge. Larger quilts will have to be rolled tightly. Slide the rolled end through the "keyhole" of the sewing machine.

5. Begin at the top of a row. Place your hands in a triangle shape. Either lockstitch, backstitch or move the stitch length to "0" and take two or three stitches to anchor the line of stitching. Sew to the end of the row. Lockstitch, backstitch or stitch in place to anchor. Continue sewing all rows, re-rolling the quilt as needed.

To avoid puckering, always run your right hand along the back, checking before you sew.

Machine Quilting Along the Borders

1. Starting at the corner of the first border, place the needle in the depth of the seam. Anchor and "stitch in the ditch," pivoting at each corner of the quilt. Upon reaching the starting point, anchor the line of stitching.

2. Repeat with additional borders.

Binding

Use a walking foot attachment and regular thread on top and in the bobbin to match the binding. Use 10 stitches per inch, or 3.5 setting.

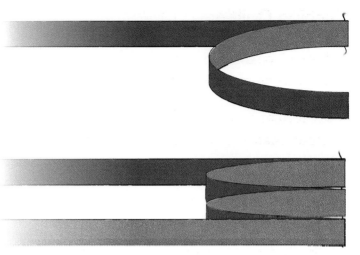

1. Square off the ends of each strip, trimming away the selvage edges. Seam the strips into one long piece. Clip the threads holding the strips together.

2. Press the binding strip in half lengthwise with wrong sides together.

3. Line up the raw edges of the folded binding with the raw edge of the quilt top at the middle of one side. Begin sewing 4" from the end of the binding.

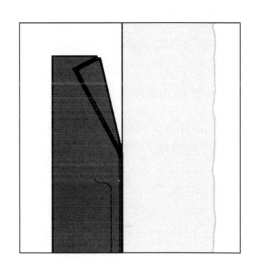

4. At the corner, stop the stitching ¼" from the edge with the needle in the fabric. Raise the presser foot and turn the quilt to the next side. Put the foot back down.

5. Sew backwards ¼" to the edge of the binding, raise the foot, and pull the quilt forward slightly.

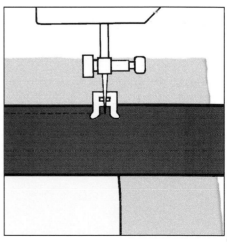

6. Fold the binding strip straight up on the diagonal. Fingerpress in the diagonal fold.

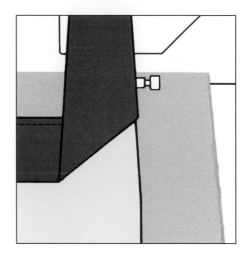

7. Fold the binding strip straight down with the diagonal fold underneath. Line up the top of the fold with the raw edge of the binding underneath. Begin sewing from the corner.

8. Continue sewing and mitering the corners around the outside of the quilt.

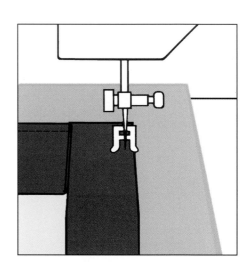

9. Stop sewing 4" from where the ends will overlap.

10. Line up the two ends of binding. Trim the excess with a ½" overlap.

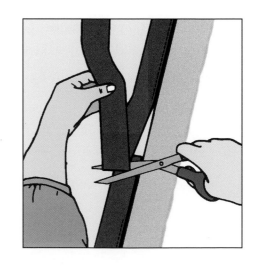

11. Open out the folded ends and pin right sides together. Sew a ¼" seam.

12. Continue to sew the binding in place.

13. Trim the batting and backing up to the raw edges of the binding.

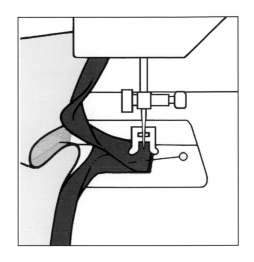

14. Fold the binding to the backside of the quilt. Pin in place so that the folded edge on the binding covers the stitching line. Tuck in the excess fabric at each miter on the diagonal.

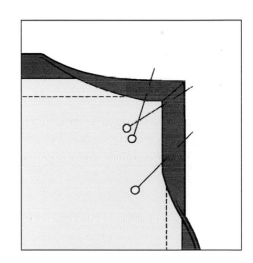

15. From the right side, "stitch in the ditch" using invisible thread on the right side, and a bobbin thread to match the binding on the back side.

Optional: Slipstitch the binding in place by hand.

16. Sew an identification label on the backing.

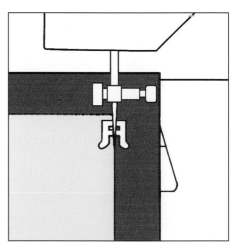

Log Cabin Tote Bag

See page 26 for supplies and cutting instructions.

1. Sew 2" strips to sides of finished block. Press seams behind strips. If necessary, trim strips to size of block.

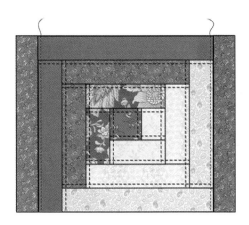

2. Pin 17½" square back right sides together to block. If width is different than 17½", cut back square and two lining squares to that square measurement.

3. Sew back to block.

4. Place on top of 18" x 32" piece of bonded batting and pin. Machine quilt or "stitch in the ditch" through the two thicknesses. Trim excess batting.

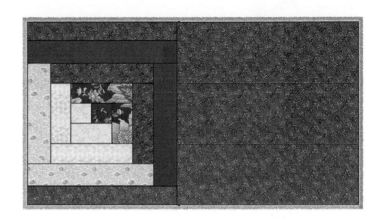

5. Handles: Fold 5" x 26" handles in half lengthwise and press. Open and press raw edges to meet in middle. Fold in half again. Edgestitch both long sides.

6. Pin handles in place 4" from the outer edges on the top right sides of the tote front and tote back.

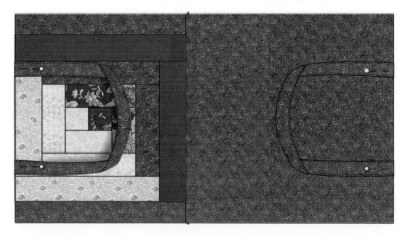

7. Lining: Cut key pockets in your desired size from scrap fabric. Sew to one lining piece.

8. Pin the lining squares right sides together to handles. The open part of the pocket faces the handle end. Sew.

9. Open flat. Turn the batting and seam allowance toward the lining. Topstitch through all thicknesses about ¼" from the edge. This is to prevent the lining from sticking out of the top of the bag.

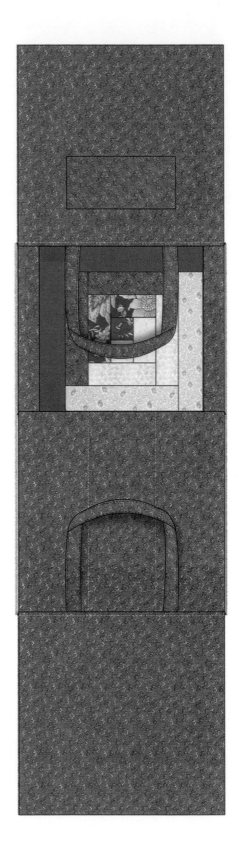

10. Refold the tote in half right sides together. Pin the seams and outside edges together.

11. Sew both long sides with a ¼" seam. Leave 6" of bottom lining open. Backstitch at dots.

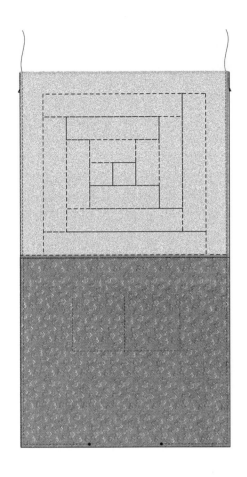

12. Reach to one corner of the lining through the opening. Push out and fold the fabric in a 45º angle. Mark a line 1½" from end. Sew on line and trim. Repeat on second lining side.

13. Sew two tote corners in same manner. Pull corners out through the lining and check from right side before trimming. Turn right side out. Sew opening shut.

14. Stitch Velcro to both sides of top for fastener.

15. Fold sides and press. Edgestitch to hold shape. Edgestitch around top.

16. Optional: Cut 3" x 14" piece of heavy cardboard for bottom.

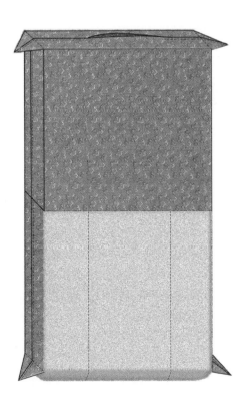

Log Cabin Pillow with Ruffle

See page 26 for supplies and cutting instructions.

1. Place the finished block on top of the batting. Machine quilt or "stitch in the ditch" through all of the thicknesses. Quilt ¼" from the seam lines for a hand quilted effect.

Many new sewing machines, such as the Elna 6003, allow you to duplicate a hand quilting stitch by using invisible thread in the needle and 60 weight cotton thread on the bobbin and tightening the thread tension to 7. Set your machine to a stitch that looks like the illustration to the right.

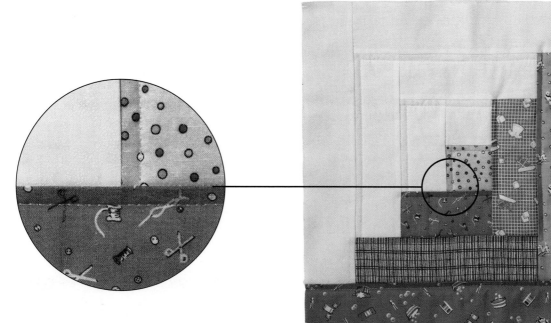

2. Ruffle strips: Sew the short sides of the 3" strips together. Repeat with the 4" strips.

3. Sew the strips together lengthwise with right sides together. Press seam to darkest side.

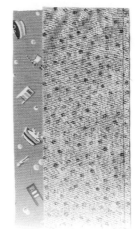

4. Fold the strip wrong sides together lengthwise. Press. Open ends and stitch right sides together so you have a continuous loop.

5. Divide the ruffle into four equal parts. Mark with pins. Cut heavy cord into four equal parts longer than each part.

6. Set your machine on a wide loose zig-zag stitch. Working on one quarter at a time, line up the cord ¼" from the raw edge on the **back side** of the strip. Zig-zag over the cord, being careful not to catch the cord while stitching.

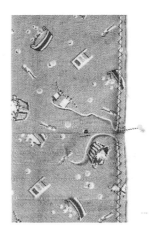

7. Draw up the cord so one quarter of the ruffle is equal to one side of the pillow.

8. With cord side up, match the raw edges of the ruffle and block. Pin the ruffle in quarters to the four sides of the block. Arrange the gathers evenly. Baste the ruffle to the pillow front.

9. Turn under and hem one 10" side of each pillow back.

10. Place two back pieces right sides together to pillow front, matching outside raw edges, and overlapping hemmed sides in center.

11. Stitch around the outside of the block.

12. Turn the pillow right side out over the 14" pillow form.

Pillow Shams

One sham holds one pillow and is made up of two blocks and 3" borders plus ruffle.

See page 27 for supplies and cutting instructions.

Blocks and Borders

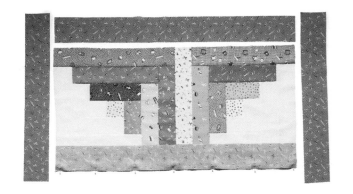

1. Sew the finished blocks together following the pattern of the quilt.

2. Cut two 3" borders the same size as the long sides. Pin to opposite sides, and sew. Press and open.

3. Repeat with borders for the short sides.

4. Center the blocks with borders on the batting, and machine quilt through all thicknesses.

Ruffles

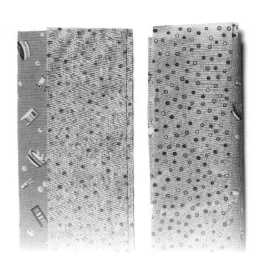

1. Sew the short sides of the 3" strips together. Repeat with 4" strips.

2. Sew the strips together lengthwise with right sides together. Press seam to the darkest side.

3. Fold the strip wrong sides together lengthwise. Press. Open ends and stitch right sides together so you have a continuous loop.

There are a number of different methods for gathering a ruffle. One method is by zig-zagging over a heavy cord.

1. Set your machine on a wide loose zig-zag stitch. Line up the cord ¼" from the raw edge on the **back side** of the strip. Zig-zag over the cord, being careful not to catch the cord while stitching.

2. Draw the cord up so the ruffle fits the sham.

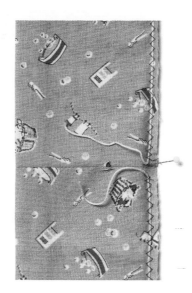

Another easy method is by simply sewing with a gathering sole, available for most machines.

1. Set your stitch length to 5.0. Tighten the top tension.

2. Run the folded ruffle under the foot. Increase the gathering by holding your finger on the back end of the gathering sole. Pile up the strip behind the gathering sole as you stitch. Release the strip after sewing every few inches.

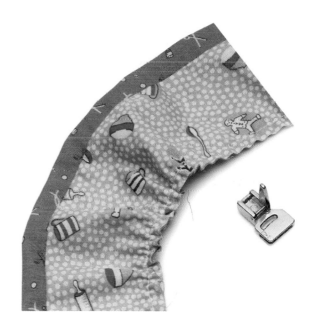

Finishing

1. Place gathered ruffle right sides together to the sham, and pin the gathers evenly around the outside edge. Baste the ruffle to the sham.

2. Turn under and hem one 19" side of each sham back.

3. Place two back pieces right sides together to sham front, matching outside raw edges, and overlapping hemmed sides in center.

4. Stitch around the outside of the sham.

5. Turn the sham right side out over a bed pillow.

Index

A

All Sevens...14, 51

B

Baby Quilt...15, 52
Backing...11, 68
Basting Clamps...71
Binding...83–85
Binder Clamps...71
Batting...11
Borders...66–68

C

Color Selection...9
Curved Needle...71, 77
Cutting...28–29

E

Extra Long Double...21, 56–57
Extra Long Twin...19, 52

F

Fabric...9
Finger Pin...62
Fiskar's Craft Cutter...28
Floss...71, 77

H

Hand Quilting...70
Hera Marker...72
History...4
Horizontal Rows...65

I

Invisible Thread...72

J

Jaws...72

K

King One...24, 56
King Two...25, 58–59
Kwik Klip...71

L

"L"...51
Lap Robe...16, 53

M

Machine Quilting...69, 79–82
Magnetic Seam Guide...30
Measuring the Bed...8

O

One Color Repeat...10

P

Paste-Up Sheet...13
Pillow...26, 90–91
Pins...60, 77
Pressing...65
Professional Quilting Service...70

Q

Quarter Inch Foot...31
Queen...22, 56–57
Quick Turn...69, 73–75
Quilt Layouts...50–59

R

Regular Double...20, 57
Regular Twin...18, 53
Rotary Cutter...28
Ruffles...91, 93
Rulers...28

S

Safety Pins...71, 76
Scraps...10
Seam Allowance...30
Serger...31
Sewing the Blocks...30–49
Sewing Top Together...60–65
Shams...27, 92–93
Shopping List...12
Square Queen...23, 58–59
Squaring...76
Squaring Up...48, 49
Stiletto...36
Stitch in the Ditch...78
Stitches Per Inch...30

T

Thread...31
Tote Bag...26, 86–89
Tying...77

V

Vertical Rows...60–63

W

Walking Foot...72, 82
Wallhanging...17, 54–55

Y

Yardage Charts...14–27

Acknowledgements

I would like to thank the following...

Benartex Fabrics, for their generous donation of the cover quilt fabrics from the Cumberland Line by Fons and Porter

And One A Day Prints on the inside back cover

My cousin, Carol Ann Selepec, who machine quilted the King size quilt shown on pages 22 and 70
She quilted it at: Amy Baughman Sewing Center
472 Constitution Blvd
New Brighton, PA 15066

Betty Bird, owner of Sew Many Ideas in Dyersburg, Tennessee, who made the Lap Robe pictured on page 16

The members of the Quilt in a Day staff who made lovely quilts for this special book:

Sue Bouchard
Sheila Meehan
Patricia Knoechel
Linda Dallman
Teresa Varnes
Luckie Yasukochi
Mary Hawkins

Don and Joanna White, for the use of their beautiful log home, located in Idylwild, California

And of course, the millions of quilters who have already made their own Log Cabin quilts.

Order Information

Quilt in a Day books offer a wide range of techniques and are directed toward a variety of skill levels. If you do not have a quilt shop in your area, you may write or call for a complete catalog and current price list of all books and patterns published by Quilt in a Day®, Inc.

Easy

Quilt in a Day Log Cabin
Irish Chain in a Day
Bits & Pieces Quilt
Trip Around the World Quilt
Heart's Delight Wallhanging
Scrap Quilt, Strips and Spider Webs
Rail Fence Quilt
Flying Geese Quilt
Star for all Seasons Placemats
Winning Hand Quilt
Courthouse Steps Quilt
From Blocks to Quilt
Nana's Garden Quilt

Applique

Applique in a Day
Dresden Plate Quilt
Sunbonnet Sue Visits Quilt in a Day
Recycled Treasures
Country Cottages and More
Creating with Color
Spools & Tools Wallhanging
Dutch Windmills Quilt

Intermediate

Trio of Treasured Quilts
Lover's Knot Quilt
Amish Quilt
May Basket Quilt
Morning Star Quilt
Friendship Quilt
Kaleidoscope Quilt
Machine Quilting Primer
Tulip Quilt
Star Log Cabin Quilt
Burgoyne Surrounded Quilt

Snowball Quilt
Tulip Table Runner
Jewel Box
Triple Irish Chain Quilts
Bears in the Woods

Holiday

Country Christmas
Bunnies & Blossoms
Patchwork Santa
Last Minute Gifts
Angel of Antiquity
Log Cabin Wreath Wallhanging
Log Cabin Christmas Tree Wallhanging
Country Flag
Lover's Knot Placemats
Stockings & Small Quilts

Sampler

The Sampler
Block Party Series 1, Quilter's Year
Block Party Series 2, Baskets & Flowers
Block Party Series 3, Quilters Almanac
Block Party Series 4, Christmas Traditions
Block Party Series 5, Pioneer Sampler
Block Party Series 6, Applique in a Day
Block Party Series 7, Stars Across America

Angle Piecing

Diamond Log Cabin Tablecloth or Treeskirt
Pineapple Quilt
Blazing Star Tablecloth
Schoolhouse Quilt
Radiant Star Quilt

Quilt in a Day®, Inc. • 1955 Diamond Street, • San Marcos, CA 92069
Toll Free: 1 800 777-4852 • Fax: (760) 591-4424
Internet: www.quilt-in-a-day.com • 8 am to 5 pm Pacific Time